The Best of
THESE DAYS

The Best of
THESE DAYS

Special Selections
from
These Days
Edited by Larry M. Correu

Published for
These Days Book Service
by
The Westminster Press
Philadelphia

Published for
These Days Book Service
by
The Westminster Press
Philadelphia

Library of Congress Cataloging in Publication Data

Main entry under title:

The Best of These days.

    1. Meditations. I. Correu, Larry M., 1931–
II.   These days.
BV4801.B43 1983   242   82-13415
ISBN 0-664-21391-X

CONTENTS

INTRODUCTION

Words from the Lord—*the Scriptures.*
Words about the Lord—*the meditation.*
Words to the Lord—*the prayer.*

Not many words, but ones carefully chosen to lift spirits Godward as the day begins, as the family eats breakfast, perhaps at the close of the day. Meditations you are glad you can save, so you can read them again and again. Meditations that speak both to your heart and to the joys and the problems of your daily life.

To select the "best" from a decade of the *These Days* devotional guide has been quite an undertaking! After all, nearly 4,000 meditations, by hundreds of writers, have been published since 1971. But select we have, to bring you the 121 meditations in this volume.

In the selection process we have given priority to helpfulness in everyday Christian living, while seeking a maximum variety in subject matter and approaches. We are well aware that many more that could not be chosen are very fine, but we are also sure that the meditations selected are outstanding.

It is with excitement, then, that we offer you this little book.

THE PUBLISHERS

DO THE NEXT THING

Simon Peter said to them, "I am going fishing."
John 21: 3.

Peter's world was smashed. His Master gone. His new life shaken. He was left alone. What to do?

In that moment old habits surfaced. An automatic system took over. He turned to what he knew, the work his hands were accustomed to doing. "I am going fishing," he said.

What to do when there is no clear lead to follow? Do what has to be done! Do what one can do. Do what lies at hand. Do your job.

This is important. Mow your lawn. Clean your house. Wash your dishes. Say your prayers. Read your Bible. Take a walk. Go fishing. Wait actively.

There is comfort in this. Silence fills with the seven demons of anxiety. Inactivity allows fear to grow into a grey, life-obscuring fog.

He for whom you search will come to you. He whom you would follow, will find you.

This is what happened to Peter. While he had his hands on the old familiar nets, standing in the familiar boat, his Master came.

Into the old patterns came a new life. Into his accustomed duties came his great friend. His Lord came to him.

Prayer: Lord, teach me how to wait, to be content with ordinary duties, unglamorous tasks, to do what lies at hand, content that you will search me out, you who are my friend and Savior, with the gift of new life. Amen.

Read Mark 12: 18–27.

PAPER-DOLLS — OR CHILDREN?

"Is not this why you are wrong, that you know neither the scriptures nor the power of God?"
Mark 12: 24.

Jesus was sure of the resurrection and the life to come. It is true that he never minimized the importance of this present life. He rarely mentioned heaven, but taught much about our motives and behavior here on earth. He even said that the whole Old Testament (his Bible) could be summed up in one short sentence, "Whatever you wish that men would do to you, do so to them" (Matt. 7: 12).

Yet belief in the life to come was the atmosphere in which all his words were set. We live under the influence of the latest headlines; he made his plans in the light of a limitless future.

And how simple were his arguments for that future. "Do you believe in the power of God?" he asked. We can imagine the future life only as an endless continuation of this present existence. We forget the power of God. In his infinite wisdom and power, God is planning a whole new creation! Again, Jesus asks, "Do you believe in the love of God?" Remember God called Abraham, Isaac and Jacob by name years after they had died. They were *still* his friends.

We are not paper-dolls that God plays with for a while and then tosses into the waste basket; we are his children.

Prayer: We thank you, our Father, that neither death, nor life, nor things present, nor things to come, nor anything else in all creation is able to separate us from your love in Christ Jesus our Lord. We pray that our love for you may be strong and unwavering. Amen.

Read Proverbs 14: 1–4.

GLORIFYING THE LITTLE DUTIES

**Where there are no oxen, there is no grain;
but abundant crops come by the strength of the ox.
Proverbs 14: 4.**

Heaven comes to those who honor God in the smallest details of their day. Brother Lawrence, one of the real saints of history, said that he could feel a divine glow in washing pans or picking up a straw from the floor.

One evening a Bible writer was cleaning his barn. Wearying a bit with this routine chore, he began to meditate. If he had no ox he would have a clean barn. But if he had no ox he would have no crop. So he set down this word of wisdom: "Where there are no oxen, there is not grain; but abundant crops come by the strength of the ox."

Suddenly he saw that the ox which caused him this nuisance was given of God to help him till his soil and harvest his crop.

Many of the bothersome little duties which sometimes irritate us could be turned to glory if we took our Lord into their doing.

Prayer: Our Father, help us to remember that heaven is right now for us whenever we do the simplest things in your divine companionship. Amen.

TAKE YOUR SHARE

**Take your share of suffering as a good soldier of Christ.
2 Timothy 2: 3.**

Take my share! I certainly will! No one is going to get what's mine! And do I ever like to receive gifts and letters and cards! After all, I'm important! I ought to get my share.

Have these thoughts ever crept into your mind about yourself? No one likes to be short-changed or gypped! So we keep our eyes open for Number One. One young mother solved this problem among her children with the wisdom of Solomon. Whenever anything is to be divided, brother carefully does the division work, but sister gets first choice. Amazing how this eliminates the arguing and fussing.

The real point is, however, that getting our share is based upon receiving all that life has to offer, as well as giving something of ourselves to others. Life offers responsibility, suffering, sorrows, sickness, and want, as well as joy and health and plenty. And it is the hard things of life which mold character and temper the spirit, and make us "good soldiers." Don't fool yourself by thinking you have the wisdom to choose. Take what God offers, and you will discover that he also sends the grace to overcome.

Prayer: O God, you send; I receive! We will share together. Give me the faith to accept the truth that you will never place a burden on my shoulders greater than you and I can bear together. In Christ's name. Amen!

Read Revelation 3: 7–13.

KEEP THE DOORS OPEN

"I know your works. Behold, I have set before you an open door, which no one is able to shut."
Revelation 3: 8.

How good it is that Philadelphia is between Sardis and Laodicea! Sometimes it seems that all congregations are like the latter two. And then we remember Philadelphia in the middle. Philadelphia is the "person" who will be the fresh spirit, the warm glow, the helping hand, the inspiring challenge to you today.

Have you ever hunted clear agates on a rocky seashore? Millions of stones of varied sizes, shapes, and colors lie before you. At first glance they all seem the same. But look more closely, carefully. And there you will find eventually a fine, clear agate; transluscent, bright, smooth—waiting to belong to you.

Philadelphia is a special agate—the church of the open door. That means not only that everyone can come in the front door, but that once they are in they find the back door also is opened wide with acceptance, new meaning, and hope for the future.

There are always those who want to shut the door, the Spirit warns. First the back door, but then the front door too, so their church can have a "nice" reputation like Sardis and Laodicea. Do not let them do it, he says, for they will be shutting the door to God.

Prayer: Dear God, help me to see the open door you have set before me for this day. In Jesus' name. Amen.

Read 1 Peter 3: 1–12.

MAKE YOUR OWN MOODS

**Do not return evil for evil or reviling for reviling; but on the contrary bless, for to this you have been called . . .
1 Peter 3: 9.**

The man worked at a job where he had to deal quite often with unfriendly people. But no matter how surly or hostile the others were, he was always cheerful. When asked how he could "keep his cool" in such situations, he smiled and said: "It's because I won't allow anyone else to dictate what my mood will be. I intend to be happy regardless of how miserable someone else might be."

How many times have your days been spoiled because you had to deal with someone or something unpleasant! The effects of all the nastiness linger long after the incidents have passed! But as the man above suggests, we can control and create our own moods, if we will.

It's human nature to be unfriendly toward someone who is cold, disaffected, or antagonistic. But if your somebody is feeling out of sorts, and you return sharp words with sharper ones of your own, you not only make the situation worse for both of you, you allow somebody else to dictate your mood!

After all, aren't there enough unpleasant situations to be faced on your own every day without inheriting the ones that other people have, too?

Why not try a little good mood making on yourself, today?

Prayer: O God, the Father of our Lord Jesus Christ, give us grace to put aside the great dangers we are in by our unhappy divisions. Take away whatever hinders us from godly peace, through Christ our Lord. Amen.

Read Psalm 9: 1–8.

DAILY WORK AND THANKSGIVING

**I will give thanks to the Lord with my whole heart;
I will tell of all thy wonderful deeds.
Psalm 9: 1.**

Sue's desk was by the window. She put her coat away and sat down with the pleasant lingering feelings of an early fall morning in her mind. Her thoughts raced as she viewed the street from her window. "Another new day; doors open for the morning: garages, elevators, truck doors, tool boxes. . . .

"Motors start, briefcases open to another day, someone says 'Good morning!' . . . Coffee perks, telephones ring, typewriters hum, hammers begin their work, glances exchange, the mail comes.

"God, what a wonderful world you have made. It is wonderful to be busy, to be needed, wonderful not to feel alone today. . . . Thank you."

Prayer: Lord, thank you for the times we feel grateful, when we can see your hand in the commonplace, the everyday. Sometimes we feel like saying "Yes" to all of life—to its pain and its joys, to its up and its downs—because it has meaning to us in Jesus Christ. Thank you for life, for *meaning* in life. God, we can say "Yes" even to suffering and to death, for you have overcome them in your Son. Thank you, God. Amen.

17

Read 1 Corinthians 13.

THE YOUNG AND CRAZY YEARS

When I was a child . . . when I became a man . . .
1 Corinthians 13: 11.

Recently students in two high schools, having made up their minds to set a world's record, did so. The winning team scored over four thousand points in a basketball game that kept a string of players running contiuously 177 hours.

Someone with gray hair exclaimed, "Crazy kids!"

Yes, but not much crazier than those kids who used to stumble around in marathon dances that went on and on, who sat for weeks at a stretch on a flagpole, or who swallowed goldfish. It may be a mark of progress, after all, that this generation has let some of the old records stand. They're young and crazy in their own way—God bless their uncut, hairy heads!

Growing older, one reflects on certain aspects of youth in disbelief or utter dismay, hardly recognizing that younger person as one's own self. "When I was a child, I *spoke* like a child, I *thought* like a child, I *reasoned* like a child." That's for sure. But the next part does not always happen. "When I became a man, I gave up childish ways."

True maturity outgrows childish pouting, whining, and grabbing, yet keeps a child's sense of wonder, and a receptive, imaginative, trusting acceptance of life.

Prayer: O Lord God, help us to grow in grace until we reach the fullness of the stature of Christ. Amen.

Read 2 Thessalonians 3: 6–12.

GETTING IT STRAIGHT

If any one will not work, let him not eat.
2 Thessalonians 3: 10b.

Large, glassy eyes in sunken sockets stared out from the hunger poster on the classroom wall. Underneath the photo appeared the question: "What can we do to help?" We had put the poster there as part of a program to raise money for the starving, and obviously it had offended some well-fed, uncaring teen-ager who had scrawled an answer across it: "Put them to work!"

How many persons assume falsely, as did the teen-ager, that the poor are poor because they are lazy and unwilling to provide for themselves? The truth is that most of them have to work ten times harder than we do in order to survive. Daily millions of mothers and fathers perform back-breaking jobs just to put a little food in their children's mouths. It can be documented that the percentage of those who could work but do not is very small.

We are so quick to quote these words from Second Thessalonians as our solution to hunger! But how willing are we to turn them around and say that those who work have every right to eat, as do their children?

Our Lord never questioned the work schedules of the hungry before he fed them. Neither should we.

Prayer: Our Father, never let us forget just how much more responsible our favored position makes us. May we be willing to pay the high cost of loving. Amen.

Read Matthew 25: 31–40.

SUPERSTARS OF THE KINGDOM

"Truly, I say to you, as you did it to one of the least of these my brethren, you did it to me."
Matthew 25: 40.

Those designated by the King as . . . "blessed of my Father
. . ." are shockingly ignorant of their record. Evidently they
kept no notes, files, books, or statistics. The story strongly
implies that they simply didn't know what they were doing.
Rank amateurs, probably; unsophisticated do-gooders, aim-
less bleeding hearts, naive idealists, simpleminded sob
sisters, softheaded sentimentalists, openhanded suckers
for every sad story in the hustlers' handbook. They never
seemed to have asked a single question about eligibility,
worthiness, or deserving. Whenever they met up with somebody in one kind of jam or another they simply put in some
caring time.

Such people take a pretty good shellacking in this bris-
tling world, but they never seem to get the message. Cyni-
cism, ingratitude, and lost causes evidently bother them not
at all. They continue to care as if the caring were an end in
itself.

It turns out, though, that somewhere along the line they
put their fingers on the pulse beat of eternity and met Christ
himself, face-to-face without knowing it. They never thought
of their Lord as identifying with the needy, so instead of
serving *for* him they served *him directly!* Dummies!

Prayer: Help us, good Master, to live with thy promise
that thou wilt indeed come to us. Amen.

Read Hosea 11: 1–9.

THE GENTLE REVOLUTIONARY

**I will not come to destroy.
Hosea 11: 9.**

A young man, a stranger, came to see me. He was a student at the university, doing a paper and wanted a minister's opinion—"Was Jesus a revolutionary?" I sensed the question was more than academic.

Upon reflection, I had to answer "yes." Jesus was a revolutionary. His was a revolution of values, a total upheaval of the way things were—and are. Jesus declared people are more important than property—persons more precious than institutions—love more valid than law—integrity more valuable than appearance—honesty more trustworthy than make-believe—peace more necessary than conflict—and life more ultimate than death. Such a lifestyle has to be labeled "revolutionary."

But one thing more. Hosea reminds us. God does not come to destroy. God's purpose is the radical reorientation of values and life-style, but because persons are precious and fragile, God's revolution—unlike most revolutions today —has about it the mark of tenderness. "I will not come to destroy," says the Lord.

Prayer: Lord, let us be stern but gentle in our judgments —firm but merciful in our discipline—impatient with evil, but merciful toward people—revolutionary in purpose, but tender toward persons. In Jesus' name. Amen.

Read Hebrews 10: 19–25.

MEETING TOGETHER

Not neglecting to meet together . . .
Hebrews 10: 25.

The readers of Hebrews are directed to meet together.

The danger of neglecting faithful, every-week meeting together lies in its effect on the life of the church and on you and me as part of the church. Absence amounts to announcing that at that moment in your life something else takes priority over the fellowship of Jesus Christ and his church. To be absent is to say, "I know Christ is in the midst of those who gather in his name, but I'll not be a party to that gathering today: I'll neither go, nor greet others there in his name, nor seek to bring another. I don't want to miss out on anything really important or of benefit, but Lord, you understand, I have other 'fish to fry' today. Count on me some other time."

What about the sick and infirm? What about vacations, oxen in ditches, business conflicts, boring sermons, family projects, those in the service, those in prison? Is it possible to be present in spirit though not in body? Yes, and sometimes this is the best answer, but how easy it is to fool ourselves into thinking this second choice is our only one when it may be an unworthy "out."

Prayer: Grant, O Lord, that I shall be among those today who can sing, "I was glad when they said unto me, 'Let us go to the house of the Lord,' " and that I shall indeed be there. For Jesus' sake. Amen.

Read Luke 9: 10–17.

DINNER—SUNDAY AFTER CHURCH

And all ate and were satisfied.
And they took up what was left over,
twelve baskets of broken pieces.
Luke 9: 17.

She was a widow with three small children. Her husband had been a tenant farmer—no insurance. She did some day work and took in ironing. They were poor so that you were afraid for them and proud so that you hurt for them.

The husband's boss donated a house, and I was going there for Sunday dinner. It had two rooms; a bare light bulb hung from the ceiling in each room. The walls had been "prettied up" with an assortment of advertising calendars, but beneath the calendars the wall paint blistered up and peeled away like corn shucks.

We had Dr. Pepper and hot dogs. You've seldom eaten so good unless you've been really wanted for the sharing of a meal. She served on the porch—chancing a breeze. I kept thinking of Christ and loaves and fish. She kept offering more—way past our fill. We visited. As I was leaving she said, "I miss my man." She looked away as if remembering something.

"But, other than that," she said, "we ain't wanting."

Prayer: O God, in the face of our desperate wants, place your peace. Allow us to live in your bounty, assured that the Son comes for us helping us to deal with our wants. Amen.

Read Matthew 14: 28–33.

THOU ART MY GOD

**For the eyes of the Lord are upon the righteous,
and his ears are open to their prayer.
1 Peter 3: 12.**

A very good reason for prayer is that God isn't restricted to "out there" in eternity but is also here and now, close to where I am—perceiving, recognizing, and responding to this little creature—me.

St. Augustine said: "O God, I thank thee for thyself." In Psalm 34 the writer couldn't contain himself any longer: "This poor man cried, and the Lord heard him." He is conscious of God's nearness in all his experience. The thought of God brings joyous abandon to life because God *cares*.

Peter tried to influence his Lord to action with force of sword and bad counsel, but more mature insight prevailed. Prayer, too, may be abused when it becomes an "order blank" to God. ("Send me what I want, God!")

As a ship comes into the harbor, hawsers are thrown to the pier for mooring. We don't pull the land to the ship but the ship to the pier. How we approach a day is determined by whether we draw near to God or whether our little self would try to move the eternal.

Prayer changes perspectives, widens concerns, humanizes persons, clarifies God's purposes.

Prayer: Father, may my prayers form me for YOU. Amen.

WHEN THERE'S NO WAY OUT BUT THROUGH

The Egyptians pursued them . . .
and overtook them encamped at the sea.
Exodus 14: 9.

On paper the plan looked good—a fast escape, a new land, a new day, a land flowing with milk and honey. There was only one hitch. No one had figured out how to get over the Red Sea! The Egyptians closed in and the end seemed near.

Sounds familiar, doesn't it? We all make plans, we dream our dreams, and then we run into a situation which seems to have no solution. We say, "This is it. I'll never make it. My loved one is gone, I cannot continue. My friends have deserted and left. My strength and resources are gone, I cannot fight anymore. I am all alone."

And then we cry out to God for help, and what happens? The waters open. A solution is provided that we never imagined. God creates out of the impossible the possible. God asks us to be careful to do the right and then leave the rest to him.

The Little Professor of Piney Woods, Dr. Laurence C. Jones, said the secret of his great success was that he prayed as if everything depended upon God, and he worked as if everything depended upon himself.

That's an unbeatable combination. Most of the time the only way out is through, but you aren't alone. God goes before. Learn to trust him to see you through.

Prayer: Lord, I believe; help me to believe more. Amen.

Read Revelation 21: 1–8.

DEATH TRIUMPHANT

He will wipe away every tear from their eyes, and death shall be no more, neither shall there be mourning nor crying nor pain any more, for the former things have passed away.
Revelation 21: 4.

The group of mourners was small. Perhaps others had felt as I—that they lacked the strength to stand at this graveside in summer's bright sunshine. We had known for a long time that Susan lived with cancer. There had been surgery, radium treatments, and drug experiments. Her body grew ravaged, but somehow one was never aware of this. There was a shining light about Susan. How trite to say she wore a halo, but she did. Oh, she wept and even cursed the pain and inconvenience, but she lived every day given to her with love. Somehow I had expected God to grant Susan a miracle. I knew the prognosis, yet I was unprepared for this moment by her grave.

The service was brief. I watched her children, calm and dry-eyed, each take a rose from the spray upon her casket. Her sister, as shaken as I, spoke. "Susan prepared them well for sorrow." Perhaps Susan was granted her miracle—time to do what she must. And now she was free of pain—her spirit soaring!

Prayer: Lord Jesus, in thy infinite wisdom grant an end to pain and sorrows. Renew our faltering faith in thy miracles and lead us to trust in thy love. Amen.

Read Ephesians 5: 1–5.

KEEP MOVING ON LOVE'S HIGHWAY

Therefore be imitators of God, as beloved children.
And walk in love, as Christ loved us.
Ephesians 5: 1–2a.

An elderly farmer was sitting with his wife on their porch one summer evening. After a long silence, he suddenly stopped his rocking and said to her: "You know, Sarah, you have meant so much to me over the years that sometimes it's more than I can stand not to tell you about it."

Paul's advice to the Ephesian Christians about "walking in love" suggests, in the original, a procession and a continuous development. It is particularly applicable to married love. He indicates that love, patterned after the love of Christ, moves from strength to strength. For those who experience it, it grows stronger as the years go by.

Love's bonds are tenuous at first. We soon learn it means drill as well as thrill. We share the joys and sorrows of the family. We enjoy the freedoms of middle age. Husbands and wives minister to one another in the sunset years. Each period has its challenges and satisfactions. For those who walk in Christ, marriage is a continuous adventure. God wonderfully uses the sunshine and shade of the years as we keep moving on love's highway.

Prayer: Lord, suffer us not to take each other for granted, but ever to give attention to the little things that redeem the ordinary and enhance the pattern of the years. Amen.

Read Luke 7: 36–50.

BEING FORGIVEN

**"Her sins, which are many, are forgiven, for she loved much; but he who is forgiven little, loves little."
Luke 7: 47.**

Who would you name "Mr. Evil" of all time? The apostle Paul?

No? Paul wrote to Timothy, "I am the worst of sinners." His record shows otherwise, of course. But note this: If Paul had not seen himself as the "worst of sinners," he could never have become the best of disciples.

Why in the world would a poor woman spend her money for $100-an-ounce perfume, and then empty it over someone's feet? It made sense, though, to this woman Luke tells of.

She and Paul—both knew they had been all wrong, and Christ's forgiveness had made them all right. It was because they had been forgiven so much that they loved Christ so much.

Check your own love-for-Christ gauge. Does it read "full"? Or only half-full—or less? Now look at your loyalty index: have you always put Christ, his work, his church, first? If yours is a "loose connection" commitment—on and off—it could be that you have never let yourself see how much you have been forgiven.

Prayer: Father, we prefer not to look at what's wrong with us; it's uncomfortable. But help us to see all of it, so we can love you as you love us. Amen.

Read Matthew 13: 31–33, 44–45, 51–52.

TREASURES OLD AND NEW

". . . like a householder who brings out of his treasure what is new and what is old."
Matthew 13: 52.

There are two kinds of people in every church. There are the "traditionalists," who want to keep things as they have always been—to sing the same songs, say the same prayers, and conduct the sacraments in the customary manner. And there are the "innovators," who want to do things in new ways—to be fresh and imaginative and experimental. This is not simply a matter of age. Some young people are traditional; some old people are creative.

A wise church tries to satisfy both these types of people. It uses old hymns, old prayers, old rituals, provided they still have value. It also experiments with new songs, new media, new forms of worship, expressing the faith in contemporary terms. People often find that an old idea takes on new meaning when it is set forth in a new and striking way. Thus the spiritual life of everyone is enriched.

A wise church is like the man in Jesus' parable. It brings out of its storehouse treasures both old and new.

Prayer: Lord, you have told us to sing unto you a new song. May I sing you a new song—born of my new understanding, my new sense of the purpose of life, my new joy in your wonder and glory! In Jesus' name. Amen.

Read Jeremiah 2: 9–13.

GOD FEEDS US

*"They have forsaken me, the fountain of living waters,
and hewed out cisterns for themselves,
broken cisterns, that can hold no water."*
Jeremiah 2: 13.

The fountain and the cistern. Jeremiah is nothing if not graphic in speaking for the Lord. No theory, no abstraction. The simplest farmer or townsman can really hear this.

Cistern. Simply a container which has to be filled, for it has no source of flowing water. And a broken one at that; leaky, cracked, faulty.

This is my life you describe, Jeremiah. How often empty, dry, broken. My heart thirsts. I go for water. There is none. My heart is parched and heavy. There is no help for me. I faint.

Fountain. Flowing, a source of running water feeds it. It is alive. It graces the garden. It refreshes the surroundings.

I want this, Jeremiah. The Lord the living source of my life. My life an extension of a great and flowing power and beauty. My life a fountain of living waters.

O the sad, echoing, tomb-like sound of a dry cistern! O the happy singing music of the flowing fountain!

Prayer: Lord, only you know why I try to live out of broken cisterns of faith. Forgive me. Open to me the flowing fountain, the inward replenishment, the outward and living sign of Jesus Christ. Amen.

Read Jeremiah 28.

IS EVERYBODY HAPPY?

The prophet Jeremiah said to Hananiah . . .
"May it be so! May the Lord indeed do this:
may he fulfil all that you have prophesied. . . ."
Jeremiah 28: 5 (N.E.B.)

Do you remember Ted Lewis? Some of you older folks may. He used to come onstage with his battered top hat, his old clarinet, and ask the audience: "Is everybody happy?" And everybody was when he got started with the entertainment.

But you know everybody wasn't happy. Beneath those elegantly coiffured heads, behind those bleary eyes, and around those dancing feet the real tears could be found! The young folks today say: "hang in there"; and they really did when Ted Lewis said those magic words—for they so desperately wanted to be happy.

But you can't do it that way. You can't go on pretending when it's not so. Hananiah thought you could. He spoke out boldly about happiness, what was coming, the enemy beaten, the former glory put back—but he died because his happiness was built on the wrong things.

Real happiness sometimes comes with tears, with defeat, with going down to Egypt with the people even though they were wrong. Jeremiah did that and because he was with them they knew he cared and they knew somehow that happiness was not fooling yourself, but telling it like it is—and that's telling it God's way. Is everybody happy? Are you? Let God in on it—you can, you know. It's up to you!

Prayer: O God, make us really happy, not because things are all OK, but because you are and we trust you. Amen.

Read Luke 19: 1–10.

HOW TO LOSE A FALSE FACE

"Today salvation has come to this house . . .
for the Son of man came to seek and to save the lost."
Luke 19: 9–10.

Luke tells you just enough about Zacchaeus to give you an idea that Zacchaeus saw himself as a small man who had a big "in" with the "in crowd" over at the capitol, a man with a good job, and at least a little wealth.

Isn't Zacchaeus a lot like some of God's gifted people today? They have such a shortened view of who they are. They're lost in a maze of notions that everything hangs on their being known as one of the "ins," or as the holder of a fat stock portfolio. Which, of course, isn't the way God sees them at all.

By the chemistry of grace something big did happen to Zacchaeus. When Jesus came to supper and Zacchaeus saw Christ and himself together, then the little man with the big "in" saw something else; for the first time he saw himself, not through his own eyes, but through God's eyes.

Zacchaeus stripped himself of the image he'd been hiding behind all those years. He became God's man for the present and for the future. That fellow with a pipeline to the capitol became the compassionate person God meant him to be, making restitution for injustices he'd felt compelled to commit while wearing that false face.

Prayer: Dear Lord Christ, have supper with us, and open our hearts that we may have some glimpse of ourselves through God's eyes. Amen.

Read Psalm 23.

MY SHEPHERD

The Lord is my shepherd, I shall not want.
Psalm 23: 1.

The Lord is my shepherd. But those are such old words, so musty and distant from where I live today! I don't know any shepherds. I hardly ever see a sheep.

The Lord is my . . . my what? There must be some modern way to put it, some metaphor that comes from my life rather than the psalmist's. The Lord is my . . . my teacher? my pastor? lawyer? psychiatrist? tax consultant? No, none of those will do. None is big enough. In whose hands can I trust my life, my body and soul, my past and future, my whole being? Who can love me totally, mixed-up and inconsistent as I am? Who is wise enough to guide me when all is darkness, strong enough to lift me when all is despair?

There is no one—except the one who is beyond all others. And in my groping I turn, as the psalmist turned, to him who is the Lord and shepherd of us all.

I do not understand him very well. Often I wander away from him or turn my back. Yet even then his love enfolds me like the air that I breathe. How can I explain that? I can't. I only know that it is so.

Prayer: Father in heaven, beyond all sight, beyond all comprehension, open my eyes and my heart that I may know you as my shepherd. In Christ's name. Amen.

A TIME FOR LAUNCHING

**Thus the LORD used to speak to Moses face to face,
as a man speaks to his friend.
Exodus 33: 11.**

It did not take him long to pack. Clothes, books, treasures from childhood. Our youngest on the eve of college. Oh, the flying years! Now, standing taller than I, impatient to be off, assured yet apprehensive of the unknowns ahead. I wondered if I had ever said anything at all significant to him. Does he know we really mean our spoken love? He reassured me in three short words as he turned to leave. "Goody-bye friend," he said.

Children are indeed for launching. That is to say that through childhood and adolescence we prepare them for the adult world. How well they do in becoming persons in their own right is a process of family living no academics can replace. A successful launching may mean return countless times, but he knows he commands his own ship. Parents must be prepared to help cast off the mooring lines, offering both freedom and haven, too.

Prayer: At the time when children leave, we pray that they might feel the presence of your loving care. So help us in the launching that they can sail tall, eyes fixed on the stars. In your gracious name and for the sake of your Son we pray. Amen.

IN OUR MIDST

"If this man were a prophet, he would have known who and what sort of a woman this is . . . she is a sinner."
Luke 7: 39.

This is a true story, which happened at a wedding reception in the basement of a church where I had gone to conduct a wedding in a rural community in Kentucky.

There was a young man there, the husband of one of the attendants, who was obviously being left out of the festivities. I watched a long time as he sat, silent and alone in the corner of the fellowship hall.

I suspected the man was left alone because of his appearance. He wore blue jeans and sandals, and his hair was shoulder length. He had a beard very similar to the one in Sallman's painting, "The Head of Christ."

Trying to be sensitive to what was happening, and being a stranger myself, I introduced myself to this other "outsider" and we talked.

After awhile the young man said, "I know these people think I am some kind of a creep, but I am a drama major at the university. Next week we are doing *Will the Real Jesus Christ Please Stand Up,* and I am Jesus."

Prayer: Lord, make us sensitive to your presence in the person of other people. Come to us in others that we may respond with loving concern. Amen.

Read Acts 26: 24–29.

ALMOST IS NOT ENOUGH

Almost thou persuadest me to be a Christian.
Acts 26: 28 (K.J.V.).

Do you believe that Jesus is the Christ? I know you do. The world stood still while Agrippa wrestled with that question and that expression of confidence in his religious integrity. There are two possible ways to understand his answer.

The King James Version says, "Almost thou persuadest me to be a Christian." In that event, almost is simply not enough. You are not almost a sinner, nor almost in need of salvation. Jesus didn't almost die for you, nor is he almost the way. To be almost alive is to be dead, and to be almost found is still to be lost. In that event, Paul replies, I wish you were almost as I am—like me in every way except for these bonds.

The Revised Standard Version has it, "In a short time you think to make me a Christian!"—in one sermon, the first time I come to church, in this one meditation. In that event, Paul answers, whether in a short time or over the long haul, I wish that sooner or later you will be as I am now—except for these chains.

Prayer: Father, I'm not satisfied with almost a meal, or marriage, or job; don't let me be satisfied with anything short of salvation. And things in this world usually start on time—church, the theater, the ball game. They don't wait on me. Hurry me along to thee. Amen.

Read Ecclesiastes 3: 10–15.

AND FOR SOME CREEPS

**I have seen the business that God has given
to the sons of men to be busy with.
Ecclesiastes 3: 10.**

She'd spoiled their whole supper with her grieving. And she knew all of them had just sat there feeling miserable for her. All but that creepy brother—*he'd* probably asked for her dessert. He thought it was funny that she didn't have a date. All afternoon, hanging around with the lunacy grinning all over his face, wearing those stupid, laceless gym shoes. He'd wanted the money she owed him, and then a ride to Gus' house—all afternoon, something. He didn't need the money, and he had a driver's license.

She'd thought somebody would call, even until time for the dance to start. Then she heard him in the hall, outside her door. The creep often did that when she was studying. He'd just stand there not saying anything till she had a nervous breakdown or something. He spoke through the door, "Beth, hey look, I'd have asked you—if you weren't my sister and all." She tried to decide if he was being nice or if it was impudence. "I wouldn't have bought you flowers or nothing, but I would have called."

Prayer: O God, when we hurt, thank you for those who try to help us through it. In Christ's name. Amen.

Read Matthew 5: 1–16.

RECONCILIATION SPECIALISTS

**"Blessed are the peacemakers,
for they shall be called sons of God."
Matthew 5: 9.**

Several months ago the CBS Television News Department had an interesting advertisement. The announcer held a globe in his hand and said, "Nice world isn't it . . . but someone is always taking it apart."

How accurately these words describe the condition of so much of life in our world today. It is a world whose life is constantly ripped apart . . . continually torn and lacerated, in racial, family, national, and international relationships.

Nice world isn't it? Only in reality it isn't so nice; for it is sick and aching and hurting from too many splits by too many people, always taking it apart.

But Christ is aware of the tears in our relationships, so he has dispatched a battery of specialists to unite the divisions, mend the breaks, and heal the scars. He has sent a battery of people to put the world back together wherever it falls apart. Christ called these people PEACEMAKERS; "Blessed are the peacemakers. . . ."

Prayer: O Christ, who has dispatched your servants on a mission of reconciliation, may I be found among this group of specialists. In Jesus' name. Amen.

INSTRUMENTS HALLOWED FOR USE

**[He] . . . girded himself with a towel. Then he poured water into a basin, and began to wash the disciples' feet.
John 13: 4–5.**

It was one of those frantic mornings in the surgical ward. Two aides failed to show up. One nurse was pulled to work on another floor. Twenty-five patients, four of them post-operative from the day before, awaited their morning baths. And the surgeons would be making their rounds within an hour. In the utility room, Eva Dennis, senior staff nurse, clattered the wash basins and pitchers to prepare for morning care. Nine bed baths! How will I ever get them done? God help me, she cried inwardly.

Feeling pressured, she was tempted to skimp in her work. Just let it go with a hands-and-face wash. With a straightening of old sheets. But her first patient was an elderly, helpless man. His stained bedclothes and his skin begged for attention. She just had to take the time! Then, with the warmth of the bath water, the smell and feel of clean sheets, the smile of her appreciative patient, her thoughts suddenly clicked. Why, Jesus used these very utensils—a towel, a pitcher, and a basin! Somehow the insight transformed her work. It became a poured-out act of devotion.

Prayer: Lord, we all work with tools. Pencils, chalk, paring knives, typewriters, brooms, slide rules. Make them yours. Transform them, and us, into beautiful instruments used for you. In your name we pray. Amen.

Read Mark 5: 1–6.

DEEP DOWN INSIDE

Night and day among the tombs and on the mountains he was always crying out, and bruising himself with stones.
Mark 5: 5.

Sometimes she wondered to herself, if possibly, just possibly, she weren't going crazy.

It seemed as though the pile of diapers got higher and higher each day, the house got messier and messier, and John seemed to find fault more and more with what she did. She wondered if others felt the same way or if it was just her. Nothing was like she thought it would be when she and John were married nine years ago. At times she thought it might be nice to disappear. But then again she did not really want to do that at all. Or did she?

It scared her to think about all that went on inside her. Her feelings, her frustrations, her fears, her hatreds; they all seemed to overwhelm her. She could not help but wonder sometimes what might have been. What might have been had it not been for all four children, or their moving so far from Mother, or if she and John had never married at all. Yes, all of these thoughts scared her, made her feel guilty. But what was she going to do? They were her thoughts, sometimes. "Oh dear, Amy is crying again; what could be the problem now? "

Prayer: Loving Father, sometimes I have feelings and problems I don't know what to do about. I have tried not to think about them, but they are there. Be near me, please. Amen.

John 16: 12–15.

VIDEO AND AUDIO

**"He will glorify me, for he will take what is mine
and declare it to you."
John 16: 14.**

I recall a student's translation of our text: "He will show
who I am; what I've got to say, he will share with you."
Whatever else the student's effort says, it says this: Christ is
not locked out of our lives by invisibility, nor yet by in-
audibility. He is both seen and heard; by the Holy Spirit we
have both video and audio. Our Lord is here and now!

You meet him in meditation, and prayer, and devotion.
But you meet him also in the ordinary give and take of living an ordinary day—in its temptations and in its satisfactions; in troubles and successes; in rebellions and in rewards; in mistakes and in those rare moments of sound
judgment.

Your plans fail to come off, you stand alone, sort of
gasping, and the only prayer you can make is a wordless
groan. But just as he said, Christ is there; the Holy Spirit
shows him to you, telling you what he has to say.

You're tempted to lie; it's just that one small advantage
you want. But you're bewildered, nervous at your greed,
when suddenly the Spirit of truth shows you who Christ is,
not in the dim, distant past, but right here, right now!

Prayer: Seal us, O Holy Spirit, grant us thine impress we
pray;
We would be more like the Saviour, stamped with
his image today.

Amen.

Read Malachi 1: 1–14.

SNIFFING AT GOD

"What a weariness this is," you say, and you sniff at me, says the Lord of hosts.
Malachi 1: 13.

Dogs sniff. People do too, at least in the movies. The uppity, aristocratic lady. The pompous English butler. Or, driving along a country road, there's the smell of a skunk in the air. Everybody sniffs. And everybody agrees: "It's a skunk all right!"

Sniffing (for people, anyway) seems to carry with it the suggestion of superiority, a suggestion which—in more instances than not—is unbecoming to our humanity. Consider the case of the lady on the bus who thought the riffraff of passengers around her was responsible for an unpleasant odor. Then she discovered she had carried a sack of her *own* garbage onto the bus, forgetting to drop it in the garbage can on her way out of the house.

Sniffing at God sounds like bizarre behavior, the complete opposite of worship. Yet this kind of charge stands, as expressed through the conscience of a man named Malachi. To sniff—to scoff at God and shrug off his call to serve—or to adore and serve? Our human options remain pretty much the same.

Prayer: My Father, deliver me from smugness. In its place give me courage, and grace and love to share. Amen.

Read Luke 8: 1–3.

JESUS MADE A DIFFERENCE

**Soon afterward he went on through cities and villages,
preaching and bringing the good news of the kingdom of God.
And the twelve were with him, and also some women.
Luke 8: 1, 2.**

There is a story about a people who were given a sundial. They were so proud of it and delighted with the way it worked that they put a cover over it to protect it.

Like this sundial women through the ages have been so overshadowed and devaluated that they could not be who they were meant to be. They have been subordinated by a society which placed far more value on their reproductive abilities than on their intellectual capacities.

Jesus was not afraid to break the male dominated rules of his day or to refute prejudices toward women. He was unafraid of the ire of the orthodox when he spoke to the woman at the well or when he defended the prostitute from the crowd. Jesus came to the defense of women many times.

Little vignettes in the New Testament portray Jesus' friendship and respect for women. He talked with them and healed them; they traveled with him; women like Lydia, Priscilla, Dorcas, and Phoebe were prominent in the ongoing ministry. Women were in the Upper Room, at the crucifixion, and at the tomb on resurrection morning. What a difference Jesus made in their lives.

Prayer: We know we have participated in a society that forces unjust roles on people. Make a difference in our lives, Lord, and in our treatment of others. Amen.

Read Amos 8: 4–8. Matthew 8: 5–10.

HONEST DEALING

**Hear this, you who trample upon the needy.
Amos 8: 4.**

The brutal society in which Jesus ministered reflects a strange contrast. Many of the military career people he encountered seemed to be as concerned with maintaining a growing personal faith as sustaining military preparedness. These New Testament centurions reveal an openness to Jesus which our Lord holds up as an example for the disciples.

The horrors of My Lai reminded the world how essential compassion must be if integrity is to survive. Only a sterling conscience, empowered by Christ's presence, can produce consistent acts of mercy in the heat of battle. The nation which helps prepare its soldiers to hate evil, to love good, and to deal mercifully with the weak and defenseless has developed a "secret weapon" to promote world peace.

Prayer: "O God, our Father, Thou Searcher of Men's hearts . . . Strengthen and increase our admiration for honest dealing and clean thinking, and suffer not our hatred of hypocrisy and pretence ever to diminish." Amen.

Read Revelation 3: 14–22.

THE MENACE OF MEDIOCRITY

**"Behold, I stand at the door and knock; if any one hears
my voice and opens the door, I will come in to him."
Revelation 3: 20.**

How many persons in your congregation come just often
enough to keep up appearances, yet never volunteer or
accept any responsibility for any significant part of the
congregation's mission?

Obviously, they are not against the church. They and
their families are members. But they have cultivated the
ability to be affable while rejecting any appeal for costly
service.

John of Patmos must have had just such a one in mind as
he directed his word to the church at Laodicea. In John's
view, this sort of insolence was more maddening than open
opposition to the kingdom and could deserve nothing short
of divine repudiation. The violent hostility of a Saul of
Tarsus was not so contemptible as the trifling attitude of a
person who professed faith and then acted as if the demands of discipleship were a matter of indifference.

When Christ calls through some evident need, I point to
someone else and think: "That must be his job. Why doesn't
he get on with it?"

Jesus may be speaking to me, "Wake up! Look again.
Can't you see the name on that job? It's yours! That's my
knock. Let me in. Together, we can do it! "

Prayer: Help me, Lord, to heed thy knock. Amen.

45

Lamentations 1: 11–14.

CAN GRIEF BECOME "GOOD GRIEF"?

"Is it nothing to you, all you who pass by? Look and see if there is any sorrow like my sorrow which was brought upon me, which the Lord inflicted on the day of his fierce anger." Lamentations 1: 12.

"Good grief!" cries Charlie Brown in the "Peanuts" comic strip. The phrase is not original with him. All of us use this bit of slang occasionally.

Think though of what Charlie Brown and we are saying: Aren't the words almost contradictory? When, if ever, is grief to be called "good"? Wouldn't it be more accurate to say, "*Bad* grief," or "*Sad* grief"? But surely not "GOOD grief." Yet grief can be good.

Lamentations is in a sense dealing with grief's becoming "good grief." The inspired author hints at how. The familiar verse, "Is it nothing to you, all you who pass by?" suggests some ways:

1) Others share our sorrows; they don't just pass us by. The concern of others at a time of sorrow usually amazes us.

2) Others too have sorrows, though in our moments of grief we sometimes feel as if we are the only ones.

3) The grief process itself is healing. Tears may be the best therapy for an aching heart.

4) Then, also, God shares our sorrows. We should remember that God has a hand in what happens. And he is love. Through Christ he has provided a way that grief can become "good grief."

Prayer, Good Father, through Christ you can make grief into "good grief." Make it so for us now and always. Amen.

Read Galatians 6: 11–18.

THE TRANSPARENT MAN

**Henceforth let no man trouble me; for I bear
on my body the marks of Jesus.
Galatians 6: 17.**

I saw it happen and I still tremble when I think about it!
A little boy was at our summer camp as a welfare kid on
scholarship; he was a little devil, always in trouble up to
his neck except when he was around Jim. His eyes just
opened bigger when he looked at Jim, as though he
couldn't see enough of him.

Toward the end of camp, we were talking about the
change that had come over Sammy during the week. As
fate would have it, Jim and Sammy walked by then; they
must not have seen us because this is what was said: "Mister, I'll bet I know what Jesus looks like," said Sammy very
slowly. "I'll bet he looks just like you! Mister, have you
got just a little time for me?"

There was a deathly silence in which time stood still; no
one moved, not a second (not even a leaf stirred) and
Jim turned and in a voice I had never heard, said: "Sure,
son, sure!"

Sammy was not the only one who could see Jesus in
Jim. Jim was transparent to all of us. His witness was pure
evangelism, and we saw God through him that day.

This experience was exciting; I vividly remember it. You
can be like Jim, too—not exactly maybe—but like him too!

Prayer: O God, make me transparent so that when people
see me, they really see you in me. Amen.

Read Proverbs 17: 22–28.

LIVING IN THE PRESENT TENSE

The eyes of a fool are in the ends of the earth.
Proverbs 17: 24 (K.J.V.).

Often we seem to have a conspiracy against living in the present. Much of our time is spent worrying about the future or romanticizing about the past. Yet all we have is the present moment in which we live.

And many of us seem to have a conspiracy against living *where* we are now.

Do you remember the man who asked his minister where he could find happiness? He was told that he should go to the place where he would find a little blue flower, the "flower of happiness." He started out on a journey that took him around the world. He did not find happiness. Walking up to his own front door, he glanced down at the walk, and found the elusive little flowers blooming right there. Now he understood what his minister had tried to tell him—that happiness is not geographical. If you can't find it at home, you are unlikely to find it in any other place.

To look enviously at greener pastures in someone else's fields is foolish and futile. The wise person is the one who hears again God's word to Moses: "Put off thy shoes from off thy feet, for the place whereon thou standest *is* holy ground." (Exodus 3: 5, K.J.V.)

Prayer: Eternal God, Father of our spirits, we wait in reverence before thee. Help us use this moment in thy service. Amen.

Read John 17.

CREATION OUT OF CHAOS

As it is, there are many parts, yet one body.
1 Corinthians 12: 20.

Have you ever seen the conductor's score of a great symphony? It is amazing that from those pages flow the stirring chord of Beethoven's majestic "Fifth Symphony" or Bartok's exciting "Concerto for Orchestra."

The conductor's score is baffling to the uninitiated. There are lines upon lines of notes: woodwind, percussion, brass, strings; signs, symbols, numbers, and words in foreign languages, like *allegro* or *pianissimo*.

The blending together of this variety is the artistry of the great conductor; and so it is among Christ's church made up of churches. He does not seek slavish conformity; he does not seek bland uniformity. Rather, Christ seeks unity that will result in a symphony of love and faith.

God is a critical audience; Christ is an accomplished conductor. How well will we remember our lessons from Scripture and experience?

Well enough, it is hoped, so that we can begin to do our part and contribute to the beauty of the whole.

Prayer: O God, we give you the chaos of our divisions, that, under the brooding of your Spirit, a new creation might appear and we may be truly one. In Christ our Lord, we pray. Amen.

Read Habakkuk 2: 2–4; 3: 12–14.

THE VISION

**For still the vision awaits its time; it hastens
to the end—it will not lie. If it seem slow,
wait for it; it will surely come.
Habakkuk 2: 3.**

There are some verses in the New Testament that are older
than we thought. Martin Luther triggered a reformation with
the words, "The just shall live by faith." He got that from
Paul. But early on, Habakkuk, in his tower, had said as much.
"The righteous," he maintained, "shall live by his faith."
(Hab. 2: 4) And having been left with this strange little book
these last days, I rather suspect that Habakkuk did not say
that easily. Faith does not solve the problem of God or the
dilemma of human existence, but it is clearly a part of the
right response to it. In fact, it is good advice: "Hold steady,
look around you, keep your head up—something is going
to happen. You can count on it."

Josephine Smith said as much to me ten years ago in
Mississippi. "I told the children that a better day was
acomin'. It would be slow and they would have to wait and
suffer for it, but if they'd hold steady, they'd more'n likely
see it. That's my vision," she said, "and I believe it'll come."
Her eyes filled and she looked away. Neither of us realized
she had quoted Habakkuk. But no matter.

Things made a little more sense to me last week when I
read the old prophecy, "The earth will be filled with the
knowledge of . . . the Lord, as the waters cover the sea."
(Hab. 2: 14) Salvation will come. You can count on it.
Habakkuk and Josephine Smith told me so.

A vision: A day when Josephine and all her children will
be free, really free. How long, Lord?

Read Mark 5: 1–13.

THE AUTHENTIC QUESTION

**"What have you to do with me, Jesus,
Son of the Most High God?"
Mark 5: 7.**

We are in the check-out line at the grocery store. I can't escape her out-thrust chin. "I don't like the new book we're studying in our class. It's not spiritual. All about politics and economics. I know what I believe and I don't want anybody changing it."

Like the demented people who dwelt among the burial caves, some of us today live among the tombs of yesterday, possessed by the unclean spirits of self-concern and rampant individualism. Our unexamined prejudices are evil spirits fragmenting our society, making chaos of our lives and the lives of others, our differing kin. But if we allow him, Jesus can bring to us here and now the same calm serenity with which he made sane the madman in the country of the Gerasenes. It is manifested history, not theory, that Jesus does cast out that which is unclean; he does still the raging internal wars that rend us, and he does make us whole.

Jesus has everything to do with our civic, economic, religious, and personal lives.

Prayer: Lord, keep me from crying aloud among the graves of a dead past. Remove the stones with which I bruise myself. Unlock the chains of my enmity toward those who differ from me. Let me run to worship you. Amen.

Read Mark 15: 1–39.

DEATH

And it was the third hour, when they crucified him. And the inscription of the charge against him read, "The King of the Jews." Mark 15: 25–26.

They crucified him. Words stark as hammer blows driving a nail in a heavy beam. And stark was the scene—a man dying, soldiers bored, onlookers frightened or sad.

Who could see the divinity of a holy love in that broken body? Who could have known that he *was* a king, and more than a king? No one could have known. Only faith could know then that the center cross was a throne. He killed death for us by robbing it of its power. No one took his life. He gave it. And he gave it with a perfect completeness and obedience that encompasses us all within history.

He died for us so that we could live for him—and in him. In this bitter moment all the evil in the whole creation was focused on that solitary figure, but there was no defeating him. For all the power and intention of God was in him, also, and did prevail. And we can only wonder and sorrow and rejoice. There is so much in this event in which we see ourselves with penetrating clarity; for we could never deserve what he gives us in his death for us—life, abundant life.

Prayer: Lord, it is a bleak, yet, hopeful day—dead, but not dead; alive, but more than alive, Christ our Lord. Amen.

1 Thessalonians 5: 1–11.

SURPRISE! SURPRISE!

The day of the Lord will come like a thief in the night.
1 Thessalonians 5: 2.

There is something about a truly clever thief that most of us find intriguing. We may not approve of his profession, but we cannot doubt his skill. A good thief plans his theft, smoothly executes it, and then vanishes. The only trace of his having been present is that his victim finds something to be missing.

Perhaps it is time for us to play the part of a thief and do a little breaking in and stealing. There are lives about us that certainly need some compassionate thievery. Take fear as one example. It can be more constricting than a straightjacket and more crippling than any fracture. If any of us could break into the life of a fearful person and tenderly steal away that demon, our accomplishment would certainly be godly. Or consider guilt, prolonged grief, destructive anger. Does not someone need to exercise enough "stealthy compassion" to rid a few lives of such weighty possessions?

The kind of stealing we are discussing will take all of the skill of the professional thief and all of the love of the full-time Christian. But to pull off just one such heist in a lifetime is worth it all. For it clearly leaves the clue that "the day of the Lord has come."

Prayer: Proclaim your day through our freeing love, O God. Through Jesus, our Lord, we pray. Amen.

Read Jeremiah 31: 31–34.

THE HEART OF THE MATTER

But this is the covenant which I will make . . . I will put my law within them, and I will write it upon their hearts; and I will be their God, and they shall be my people.
Jeremiah 31: 33.

If you imagine the Old Testament to be a vast landscape with valleys and plains and hills, then these verses from Jeremiah are Mt. Everest. They stand out like a great beacon on the highest peak, illuminating all the countryside around it and casting light into areas not yet explored. Here, in this brief passage, is the promise of the New Testament, the revelation of grace to come.

What is new about the new covenant? Not the law for the law of God is the law of love and that does not change. It is we who are new. We become new when that law is written on our hearts. When we internalize the love of God, making it part of our inner selves, it motivates our lives. As we move and breathe and have our being—with every beat of our hearts—we live the love that is God's law for us.

The new covenant is still and continually new. It will re-awaken and revitalize us as often as we open ourselves to God's promise in Christ Jesus. God's love is a matter of the heart and that is the heart of the matter.

Prayer: God, make us part of your new covenant. Write your law upon our hearts that we may have the vision and perception which come when your love is within us. Grant us grace that we may be created anew in the spirit of your Son, our Lord. Amen.

Read Luke 5: 1–11.

CAN YOU SAY, "YES"?

And Simon answered, "Master, we toiled all night and took nothing! But at your word I will let down the nets."
Luke 5: 5.

Wouldn't you like to be a part of a church where the people are not afraid to risk, to dream, to say *yes,* to let in a little fresh air?

When Jesus asked Simon Peter for the use of his boat, Peter could have replied, "Sorry, but we've been fishing all night and we're dead tired—some other time." Instead, Peter pushed his boat out and held it steady while Jesus taught. After Jesus had finished he told Peter to push out into the deep and for them to let down their nets, and when they did this their nets were so full they started breaking.

Christ's requests often come to us when we are tired or have other priorities. But, if we are taking seriously the message of Jesus Christ, if we are willing to say *yes*—then we will throw open our doors for that fresh air of spiritual adventure to come in. It could change the course of our lives. It changed Peter's life from the business of fishing for fish to the calling of fishing for persons. As we worship and serve in the church, a believing fellowship, how exciting it can be to experience the adventure of being alive and at work in ministry to the needs of people.

Prayer: Our Father, create in us the spirit of adventure and the courage to say *yes* to you. Amen.

Read 2 Corinthians 5: 16–21.

JAN

**He is a new creature: old things have passed away;
behold, all things are become new.
2 Corinthians 5: 17 (K.J.V.).**

Have I lost myself in my husband's career?

The years since we were married have been spent in one continuous climb to get "there." We wanted to achieve comfort and security. We worked for our goal together. What do I do now that we have "arrived"? The struggle to get to the top of life was our struggle—his and mine. We sacrificed, endured, dreamed, and waited. Now that we have our comfort he no longer needs a co-worker.

My husband needs a different wife in me now. He has changed; I must change too. To say that all we have worked for through the past years in itself is no longer enough to be fulfilling sounds thankless and selfish. I need personal goals. I need to reorder my life and begin to find who I am again. To become lost in the identity my husband claims is neither satisfying nor healthy. I must find a new part of me—the woman he needs now and that I can be now.

From where does this new woman emerge? What resource can produce someone that is hidden even from me? How does one start to become a new, different, and fuller person?

Prayer: Loving Father, it is difficult to change; we are comfortable with things the way they are. When we feel that you are calling us out of our nesting places, we become frightened. Please help us to become what we were meant to be. Amen.

Read Psalm 71: 9–14.

THE BEAUTY OF THE SUNSET

The glory of young men is their strength, but the beauty of old men is their gray hair.
Proverbs 20: 29.

We have really blown it! In coming to this cult of youth worship, what is there for a young person to anticipate if we live as though there is nothing attractive past the early years? We are extending the human life span with each generation, but at the same time, we seem to be insisting that the apex of a person's life has to come at a younger and younger age!

People are not like equipment or merchandise that is to be thrown away when it gets old. Just like anything that has the ring of quality to it, people should be more valuable as they get older. Someone has said that real wisdom is what you learn after you know it all. That's worth something, and it only comes with experience. Then too, the signs of wear that appear on the body are some of the best beauty marks to be found.

Those marks tell a quiet story of responsibilities that have been faithfully handled, of grief and disappointment that have been carried creatively, of some battles that have been won and some that have been lost. They are the evidence of a person living an exposed life, and should be shown proudly. The sunset is as beautiful as the sunrise.

Prayer: Our Great Creator, you have made all things beautiful in its season. So we thank you for age, and pray that we may hold in honor all who have graciously come to the winter of life. Amen.

Read Romans 14: 10–15.

SOCIAL PAIN

**Then let us no more pass judgment on one another, but rather
decide never to put a stumbling-block or hindrance in the
way of a brother.
Romans 14: 13.**

"Any physical pain I suffer because of my disability is quite
insignificant in comparison to the social pain I live with all
the time—the pain of being treated as somewhat less than
human because I cannot walk and talk like other people."
Susanne Moss was explaining why her recent book is titled,
Too Many Tears.

"I have learned to live with my deafness," an attractive
university student told me. "What bothers me most is the
fact that many people treat me as if I were a simple-minded
child."

"You may be engaged to one another if you wish," a
cerebral palsied young couple were told. "But of course you
can never marry."

Dr. Jean Vanier, friend of all handicapped persons, coun-
sels us to "listen to the heartbeats of their existence." We
do not have to listen very hard these days to hear the rising
tide of their indignation.

"We can feel—we can love—we are whole persons! When
you evaluate us only in terms of one obvious disability, you
add more painful handicaps than those with which we were
burdened initially."

Prayer: Forgive us, our Father, for adding to the burdens
that others carry, when you have commanded us to bear
one another's burdens. Amen.

Read Genesis 35: 1–4.

THE QUALITY OF GRATITUDE

"Then let us arise and go up to Bethel, that I may make there an altar to the God who answered me in the day of my distress and has been with me wherever I have gone."
Genesis 35: 3.

A minor medical check-up revealed the possibility of something deadly, and never had the days passed so slowly until a wonderful lab report erased the problem. That was a moment I had dreamed about and the next Sunday I wanted all the trumpets and hallelujahs the church's worship service offered. But a shortage in the church school staff required me to assist with the junior church service. How resentful I was not to be up in the vaulted sanctuary singing my heart out! Then I heard the reedy voice of a child say, "We thank you God for everyday," and my heart rose like a balloon in a March wind.

As I bent my head for the simple prayer that followed, I realized that in this world our Father made every small prayer is as mighty as an orchestra, every acknowledgment of our Maker as beautiful as birth itself, and every gentle thought a psalm. Sincerity does not need to shout. As usual, with God's way, out of fear came learning; out of worry, strength. I lift my spirit with the thought that there are no small thank yous.

Prayer: Dear God, it is so easy to talk of taking adversity with faith until the searing moment one is tested. Help me know with every fiber of my being that I always walk hand in hand with you, no less in joy than in fear or sorrow. Amen.

Read Genesis 36: 6–8.

THE RESPONSIBILITY OF PLENTY

For their possessions were too great for them to dwell together; the land of their sojournings could not support them because of their cattle.
Genesis 36: 7.

"If hungry children want my spinach, send it to 'em," the child said angrily. And because they had never known hunger, the family repeated that remark with much laughter. Clearly, the starkness of international food conferences, the long, sad deaths on the desert, and the terrible effects of malnutrition in those unlucky enough to live have not yet touched the well-fed.

"Let's raise money to send food," came from the teenagers who were touched by films of bloated-bellied babies. And so they organized, promoted, collected. The results, however, were disappointing. Too much inflation, recession, other obligations, etc.! Yet the congregation wanted to hear a report on the campaign and asked for a representative of the young people to speak for a few minutes during the Sunday worship service. A gangly youth made his way to the pulpit and announced the tally. "The money collected," he said simply, "amounted to thirty pieces of silver."

Prayer: Dear Master, you weep to see your children suffer, but do more tears flow when one person will not help another. I do not criticize the comfort we enjoy, only that I have done so little for those who live in desolation. Give me the guidance to help constructively. Amen.

Read John 1: 1–18.

THE WORD

And the Word became flesh and dwelt among us, full of grace and truth; we have beheld his glory, glory as of the only Son from the Father.
John 1: 14.

The most magnificent, mind-boggling thing has happened! The Immortal, Invisible God has become mortal, visible, tangible, and we have beheld his glory, a glory surpassing all imagination. To this Creator of the cosmos, space and infinity are no mysteries; all things inanimate and alive must trace their origin, sustenance, and destiny to this power.

Let me tell you about him, though if all were written that could be written about him there would not be room in all the world to contain the books. But let me try to tell you at least something.

In him is life that shows what a person can become. He brings to humanity a new degree of radiance. He is so good there is no accounting for him but to concede that he is divine. A part of our consternation arises from the lack in him of what we had supposed was the indispensable clothing of majesty. We claim him as Lord and Master, but he doesn't "lord" it over us. For all his being so wonderful, he is not acclaimed by his own people. His radiance bursts forth in deep darkness, but the darkness is unable to extinguish it. His radiance is the very unveiling of the nature of the Eternal. It is the offer to *us* of the power to become what he calls us to be: children of God!

Prayer: O Lord, open our hearts to thy glory. For Jesus' sake. Amen.

Read John 18: 37, 38; 1 Peter 2: 22.

I AM A PHONY

There was no deceit in his mouth.
Isaiah 53: 9.

I have always wanted to think of myself as being a sincere person. Real. Genuine. No hypocrite. Not superficial. But I am not. I am a phony. In a phony age. Not real, not true. Not what I would appear to be. Confessing to be but not really being. I am a sinner, a phony, always missing the mark. Always settling for second-rate values, the cheap, the current, the contemporary. A stuffed shirt. No? Am I really like this? Yes. For none of us makes it to perfection. We know what is right but do not do it. We are at best sinners, saved by grace.

But that does not mean I am satisfied with this status. I really want to improve. I want to be more genteel, more whole. More of the same substance. Pure in heart. Christ, my example and savior, both shames and challenges me. I see my failures. But I look at him and want to be more like him. The amazing thing about him was the wholeness of his life. His teachings and his life were one, like the seamless robe the crucifiers gambled for. He was all of one piece. Integrity is the word for it. If I can just get closer to him, touch him, or let him touch me, I believe some of his integrity can become mine.

Prayer: O Christ, the only truly real person this world has ever known, forgive me for my sham. Make me deeply dissatisfied with it. Heal me with your health and wholeness. Amen.

Read Luke 15: 11–24.

LORD OF EMBARRASSMENT

"Father, I have sinned against heaven and before you; I am no longer worthy to be called your son."
Luke 15: 18–19.

From some brain cranny comes a story about a tot who put his knee through the lace curtain. He looked at the knee-sized split and said, "I wish I was the hole, and the hole was me." O to be anybody or anything besides himself!

But his mother didn't want him to be anybody but himself. She took him for who he was and loved him in spite of what he'd done. Which is what forgiving does; it clears the way for you to come to yourself and to be yourself again. It also helps you let God's other people be themselves, too.

Trouble with us—when we come a cropper, we crawl into a hidey-hole and nurse and pick at our embarrassment. If we stay long enough, pride throbs against everybody else, and we even begin to blame mother for putting the curtain up in the first place.

Do you know what the doctor says about picking at wounds? "Don't! Clean! Patch! Forget them!" I wonder if that may not mean, "Forgive them!" If mother and God forgive you, who are you to clutch the knee-sized hole to yourself?

Prayer: Dear God, whose forgiveness is from the foundation of the world, if I have done much wrong grant that I may balance it by doing something good. But at any rate, if I have my neighbor's and my God's forgiveness, let me forgive myself! Amen.

Read Philippians 3: 12-16.

ONE DAY AT A TIME

Forgetting what lies behind and straining forward to what lies ahead.
Philippians 3: 13.

One of the first things my recovering alcoholic friends said they did was live one day at a time. In the past when I would quit drinking it would be "forever." This was too much for me to handle but I found out that with the help of God I could make it for *one day.* Sometimes I have to narrow this down even more and concentrate on living in the "now." The present *moment* is all that I have any power to control.

Paul's example and words have helped me forget the past and not feel guilty. A little rational thinking has also helped me with my guilt. It is easy to ask: if the past is so important, why hasn't God seen fit to go back and change some things that happened? But if I dwell on the past, I am putting myself above God, trying to deal with something he doesn't bother with. If I choose to feel guilty I am also saying that Jesus died for everyone but me. He died for my sins so I would not have to carry the burden of guilt that he knows is too much of a load.

I can plan for tomorrow but when I begin projecting into the future, wondering "what if," I am replacing faith with fear. Living this one day with God's help keeps me sober.

Prayer: Dear God, thank you for loving me so much that you do not put more on me than I can stand and thank you for your son, Jesus who died to set me free from guilt. Amen.

Read Nehemiah 5: 1–13.

PERSONS BEFORE PROFIT

There came a time when . . . Some complained that they were giving their sons and daughters as pledges for food to keep themselves alive.
Nehemiah 5: 1 (N.E.B.).

In the novel *Airport* a man worried over his debts takes out a large insurance policy on his life, then attempts to arrange his death by a bomb carried onto a plane.

That the sale of life, that every sort of slavery, violates something deep in our sense of right and wrong, is obvious. Nothing is as precious as a person.

Yet, in the everyday world of work, persons still frequently come off second best. Employees, customers, secretaries, salespersons, even "the boss" become just roles that are played. The persons and their life-worlds and needs are somehow lost to us. Or, while we are usually not guilty of mortgaging our children's lives for money, we may exchange the chance to enjoy them for a string of "urgent meetings."

Our belief in work has helped us to clear forests, build shining cities, and automated homes. Work is part of our strength, and we are not ashamed of being those who have not been afraid to work. But fancy incomes, and progress up the success ladder are not worth it if these cost us time and love for each other.

Prayer: Help us, O God, to discover the living Christ in each other, and to turn each personal relationship that fills our days into an opportunity to widen our horizons and to share ourselves. Through Christ. Amen.

Read Matthew 26: 26–29.

THE FACE OF THE ONE YOU ARE

My sin is ever before me.
Psalms 51: 3.

But as you look more intently into the communion cup, a particular face presses into view. As it takes more definite form, you become aware that you are looking at your own face. If you are frank with yourself, you will see there:
—not the one you pretend to be
—not the one others think you are
—not the one you would like them to believe you are
BUT THE ONE YOU ARE
with all your weaknesses, your shortcomings, your faults.
And as you ponder that face, there comes back to you:
—the temptations that were too much
—the words you would like to take back
—the deal that you are ashamed of
—the time when you compromised instead of standing firm
—the wrong that you didn't right.
Yes, there are people who think you are good but they may not know the person struggling inside you. Truly, as you look at yourself mirrored in the cup, you are not altogether proud of what you see . . .

Prayer: Dear God, hear my confession. I withhold nothing. In Jesus' name. Amen.

Read Genesis 1: 26–29.

THE FACE GOD CALLS YOU TO BE

God created man in his own image.
Genesis 1: 27.

As you gaze into the communion cup there looms behind the person you are—another. You discover it is the face of the person God calls you to be. You see there one of
  —clean mind and pure heart
  —upright and dependable
  —gracious and kind
  —sincere and honest
  —humble and compassionate.
You see there a person of Christian character, of faith and hope. For deeply buried in everyone there is another that God would fashion.

A story that went the rounds years ago concerned Andy, an old Indian in the interior of Canada near a railroad camp. Daily he was seen busy whittling at an old railroad tie. Then one day, he lifted it up and there stood a stalwart Indian brave. "Why, Andy, how did you ever do it?" an onlooker asked. Replied Andy, "He there all the time. Andy just whittle him out."

Prayer: O God, we thank thee for the image of thyself planted within us, waiting to be "whittled out." Help us, we pray, to hear Christ's call to be like him. In his name. Amen.

Read 1 John 1: 5–10.

THE YOU IN ECUMENICAL

**If we live our lives in the light, as he is in the light, we
are in union with one another.
1 John 1: 7 (Jerusalem Bible).**

The most desperate feelings we have are when we feel
utterly alone. We react this way because God made us to
love being together. We are more human, more whole,
more happy when we are in the midst of and loved by
people.

God made people for NEARNESS. He came that we might
receive the gift of community. His gift causes congregation;
creates church; blesses family and celebrates community.

The ecumenical urge is Christ's drive to create unity for
a broken world. In Christ, people and groups, even de-
nominations, hunger to come together and to enjoy one
another. This is the will of God for health and wholeness,
and it cannot be thwarted.

His love linked to his power will enable us to blast
through custom, ancient dogmas, and our stunted selves to
clasp the brothers and sisters Jesus has given us.

When that happens, the event at the heart of church
unity has happened. All the rest is postlude. The proud
names used now to divide us into camps of indifference
and even suspicion will wither and die. Unity is coming. He
wills it.

Prayer: Loving Father, we are hostile and afraid of some
of our brothers and sisters in the church. What divides us?
Who keeps us apart? Make your church whole that people
may believe in your Son. In his name. Amen.

Read Matthew 7: 1–12.

BROTHER, ARE YOU SAVED?

"So whatever you wish that men would do to you, do so to them."
Matthew 7: 12.

Once while serving as a Christian missionary in Japan, I was buttonholed by a follower of one of the "new religions" there. He knew I had a faith strong enough to bring me from my country to his, but he had no interest in my views. He had his book, and he had all the answers. It was thoroughly unsettling to find myself the object of his attempts at conversion.

Perhaps that experience taught me more than any book or saintly teacher could have about the way to show people the love of God—or the way not to.

A person of another faith, or no faith, may have questions about my religion, or some about his own. He may be a "satisfied atheist" right now. But whatever his position, I must offer him the courtesy of respecting him as a person.

Prayer: Father of all the human race, enable us to look beyond the labels we put on people to your presence in each one. As they are precious to you, let them be so to us. Forbid us to see any of your children as things, or just as "sinners" to be "converted." Let us learn to love with your love. For Jesus' sake. Amen.

LOVE OTHERS

A new commandment I give you: love one another. As I have loved you, so you must love one another.
John 13: 34 (T.E.V.).

"LOVE ONE ANOTHER." Love the baby, precious and sweetly dependent; love the absent child, doing well in college, making friends; love the retired parent, self-sufficiently traveling or vigorously doing volunteer work; love the life-long friend whose affection and encouragement remain constant. Love the lovable.

JESUS SAID, "LOVE ONE ANOTHER." Love the deformed baby whose eyes stare without recognition; love the defiant child whose words hurt, whose actions trouble; love the childish parent, peevishly resisting needed help; love the one-time friend with whom you do nothing but disagree. Love the unlovable.

JESUS SAID, "I HAVE LOVED YOU ..." Love *you*, wanting me to be your life, rather than to live my own; love *you*, far away, never writing or calling or coming; love *you*, hating and hurting others; love *you*, not even liking yourself.

JESUS SAID, "LOVE AS I HAVE LOVED ..." Love with steadfastness for the insecure; love with hope for the desperate; love with faith in those who disappoint; love with acceptance for those who resist love.

Prayer: Lord, help us love ... all others ... as you ... love us. Amen.

Read Psalm 121.

ALWAYS AVAILABLE

My help comes from the Lord, who made heaven and earth. Psalm 121: 2.

After twenty-three years of an enduring and happy marriage, my husband disappeared. He became the victim of a senseless and unsolved killing. The mandatory waiting period for filing a missing persons' report was fulfilled. With a sense of relief I dialed the number to set in motion a search. In amazement I heard, "That desk is closed. Please call back tomorrow."

As my children and I clung to each other, I gathered my strength as those powerful words filled me: "Behold, he who keeps Israel will neither slumber nor sleep." (vs.4) There is One whose desk is NEVER closed.

Prayer hymn: Other refuge have I none;
Hangs my helpless soul on Thee;
Leave, ah! leave me not alone,
Still support and comfort me.
All my trust on Thee is stayed,
All my help from Thee I bring;
Cover my defenseless head
With the shadow of Thy wing.
Amen.

Read 2 Corinthians 13: 11-14.

BALM OR BOMB?

**For they sow the wind, and they shall reap the whirlwind.
Hosea 8: 7.**

In Bedford, England, a husband had engraved on his wife's tombstone, these words: "Perfect Peace—Until we meet again."

Are things calm and pleasant until you appear? True, in certain situations we cannot sit quietly by and let evil take over or sin prevail. We must cry out in love, and mercy, and righteousness, and justice. But does peace reign in your home until you return? And how about your church, is the meeting peaceful until you make your appearance? In your married life does your presence mean peace, or are you a chronic nagger?

In order to be an effective witness for Jesus Christ there must be perfect peace within us. We are called to help bring order out of chaos, reconciliation instead of hatred, and courage in place of disorganization and defeat. Is it your usual practice to sow the winds with discord and hate until you and others, unfortunately, have a fullblown whirlwind on your hands? Never let it be said of you, and said with shame, that all was joyful here until you came.

Prayer: O God, may we learn the virtue of patience and of a persistent kindness that ever works to right the wrongs in our lives and in our world. Amen.

LET PEOPLE ALONE

Perceiving then that they were about to come and take him by force to make him king, Jesus withdrew again to the hills by himself.
John 6: 15.

Greta Garbo's famous remark, "I want to be alone," points to the need in everyone's life for privacy. This need can be especially crucial when things are piling up. There are moments when we just have to get away from the pressures and the people around us. The Gospels record that Jesus, who felt the need to court the company of friends, also had times when he withdrew to be by himself.

We may be most helpful to others when we do not bother them. Instinctively, when people have burdens we want to rush in to lend a hand. We have such great advice to offer! But perhaps the best thing we can do is let them lick their wounds in private. People need time to sort out their feelings without undue influence. They must be granted a certain confidence that they can handle their own problems. There is, to paraphrase Ecclesiastes, a time for socializing and a time for solitude.

The elderly have a right to be alone without overwhelming them with "things to do"; a housewife has a right to be alone without the neighbors gossiping that she has become eccentric; young people have a right to be alone without parents nagging them to get out of their room and socialize. We may love others best by granting them breathing room.

Action for the day: I will think twice before rushing in to help.

Read Judges 3: 12-30.

EHUD

**The LORD raised up for them a deliverer, Ehud, the Son of Gera, the Benjaminite, a left-handed man.
Judges 3: 15.**

I wonder if Ehud felt a little mixed up sometimes—a left-handed man from a tribe whose name meant Son of the Right Hand? It must have been a cause for joking among his neighbors. Poor Ehud.

But this misnamed man would be useful one day. Eglon the Fat met his death because no one thought to look for a two-edged sword strapped to Ehud's *right* thigh. This left-handed man was just the one needed to deliver God's people, even if his method is questionable to us today.

In our Christian land, most of us look alike. We belong to the same "tribe." It's an age of conformity when even the non-conformists look strangely alike.

But the Christian is a child of Ehud. If we are trying to be true to Christ, sooner or later we'll disarm the world with the unexpected.

Sometimes it's with honest candor when society expects us to live the polite lie. Or perhaps it's with compassion when the world has self-righteously chosen to look the other way in the presence of need.

We may seem like our right-handed neighbor, but if we are loyal to Christ, we are different. As he once put it, we are "in, but not of, the world."

Prayer: If you have work for my left hand today, Lord, please guide it and make it steady. Amen.

Read Leviticus 13: 45-46.

CHARLES

"Unclean, unclean."
Leviticus 13: 45.

I shall never forget the letter and the chilling message—Charles is dead. They found him in a motel just out of town. "An overdose of sleeping pills." I had known him since we were children and had followed his career.

Charles was a homosexual. Not many knew, but there were always rumors. Even so, it was mostly a secret. There were no accusers.

Who can say what finally "did Charles in" and who dares moralize about him? The Church has not dealt with the question. Only recently have we begun to speak sensitively about the reality. Unfortunately, like the lepers of old, Charles and his kind would be considered unclean. Feelings run deep and in the process many people suffer the pain of ostracism and rejection. Often, like Charles, they languish and die.

I do not know if the Church will ever be reconciled to the issue. A friend of mine argues that whatever may be right or wrong with us, we are the hope of God in the world. I am convinced that we must insure the rights of all men and women, for justice has to do with the loving and caring of one another, no matter how different we may be.

Prayer: O God, is it true that with you nothing is unclean or ever lost? Open our hearts to the meaning of your love in the lives of those who differ from us. Amen.

Read Matthew 5: 13; 2 Timothy 4: 6-18.

EXECUTIVE CHOICE

**"If the salt has lost its taste, how shall its saltness be restored?"
Matthew 5: 13.**

A friend of mine was 52 when he got the word that he should begin looking for another job. He had thirty outstanding years with the company, if the plaques on his wall were any indication. No reason was given for the sudden shift of loyalties except that a new policy mandated making way for younger, more versatile people.

Like all great themes, the meaning of justice, or lack of it, comes alive when it is personalized. I am appalled by the number of businessmen and women in my community who are no longer "of use to the corporation," who have lost their salt, as it were, and are so easily pitched out in this throw-away society of ours.

I am not trying to give a new interpretation to this lesson in Matthew except that sometimes, in our haste, we throw away people who are not finished yet, who still have everything to give. It takes a long time for salt to lose its savor.

A thought: How many people can you think of who have been put aside by business and industry? Maybe you are one of them. In St. Louis there is a group of former executives who are pooling their resources to help one another find new opportunities.

Read Jeremiah 7: 1-15.

MOVING OUT

"Do not trust in these deceptive words: 'This is the temple of the LORD, the temple of the LORD, the temple of the LORD.' "
Jeremiah 7: 4.

Can you imagine yourself trying to find security by chanting, "The church, the church, the church"? Or if you're Canadian, by repeating the name of your nation till you're blue in the face? Or if American, by saying, "Columbia, Columbia, Columbia," till the cows come home? That's roughly what Jeremiah saw the people around him doing with the Jerusalem temple. (See key verse above; the temple implied the nation Israel as well.)

Now we may not be able to see ourselves in Jeremiah's exaggeration. But is it possible we're there anyway? For all religion has an inward thrust that tends to unnerve the equally important outward one. We're meant to find ourselves in the outgoing process of self-giving. Security is waiting to be discovered in reaching outward. Yet how many of us church-goers can truly say we're not preoccupied with our "buildings, bucks, and bodies"?

The worlds of religion and patriotism are small enough that you can almost measure their square footage. Beyond them lie risk, dizziness, mystery, to be sure. But our faith dares us to trust that a big God with a strong arm wants to show us a grand time OUT THERE too.

Prayer: God of pilgrims past and present: convince us that worship and service go hand in hand, as our Lord has taught us. Amen.

Read Jeremiah 12: 1-6; then 11: 18-23.

IF GOD, WHY SUFFERING?

**Why does the way of the wicked prosper? Why do all who are treacherous thrive?
Jeremiah 12: 1.**

A four-year-old died recently. In cold blood her own parents had beaten her to death. Hour after hour the little girl had to run from one to the other to receive their blows afresh. No food. Stark naked. Doused in ice water. And all this before the eyes of her brothers and sisters.

"Why does the way of the wicked prosper?" Jeremiah demanded to know of God. "Why do all who are treacherous thrive?" What prompted the question for the prophet was the discovery that his own family was plotting to kill him. But so many things seem to raise the same question for us these days. Our world has all but gone berserk.

Why, God?

The answer: NONE. What could you say to an innocent child as he or she is being pulverized by the very ones who gave the child birth? What could you say that wouldn't leave the taste of gall upon your lips? *And yet a kind of answer*: one is coming who will disembowel evil in the raw. One has come, descending into hell to know the nothingness of death. A womb was emptied so that God might suffer with us. A tomb was emptied so that suffering should see defeat.

Prayer: Even so, come back, Lord Jesus. Ransom captive everything. Let it be done! Let it be done! Amen.

Read Jeremiah 14: 17-22.

CALLED TO LIFE

Why hast thou wounded us, and there is no remedy?
Jeremiah 14: 19 (N.E.B.).

Lightning struck one summer night and ignited one of the four small spires atop the church my father served in a coastal town in Maine. The next morning we were awakened by the telephone. In tears, the caller related how each morning she had looked from her window for those spires. The sight brought such comfort. Now, with but three left, she could hardly bear to face the day.

A mortuary passes out to grievers a small pamphlet. On the back is the legend, "At Peace." Unwittingly, the mortuary has made the right connection. Too much peace of mind, too easy a comfort, has more to do with death than life. There is a comfort which truly strengthens us, and there is a comfort that cushions us overmuch, so that we miss the needed stings and pricks of the spirit.

What kinds of events are breaking the cushion I may wrap around myself? Could God be using these to call me to encounter Jesus Christ afresh? To a courage I have buried? To a common cause with those whom this world brutalizes? To a new knowledge of his ministering Spirit? To a mighty hope? If God shatters a stagnant peace, may he not be offering in its place a renewed life?

Prayer: God who calls us to life, lead me, and lead your church, toward the peace built upon thanksgiving, obedience, and a hearty trust in your ways. In Christ's name. Amen.

Read 2 Samuel 12: 1-7, Mark 10: 17-22.

GIFTS THAT HURT

"You lack one thing."
Mark 10: 21.

"You have not been honest with us or with yourself."

"What you did was very wrong!"

"This is a difficult task. You are simply not ready for it."

Some "person gifts" that come to us are unpleasant and hurtful. They may anger us or make us uncomfortable because they question our attitudes or assumptions. They may cause us grief or pain because they condemn our actions, or lack of them. They may force us to be truthful with and about ourselves.

Though we may not wish to accept these gifts at the moment of delivery, we become gradually aware of their importance to us. In time we may be able to see the gift of love that is enclosed, a gift which brings us new opportunity for self-understanding, honesty, and growth.

These unpleasant "person gifts" are important. They are God's love gifts to help us grow.

Cherish them. Learn from them. Grow through them.

Prayer: We are grateful, O God, for persons who help us to see the effects of our attitudes and actions, who confront us with the realities of life. Help us not to let hurt blind us to the gifts they bring. Amen.

Read Matthew 26: 6-13.

APPRECIATION

"For she has done a beautiful thing to me."
Matthew 26: 10.

Penny is one of the most gifted persons I have met. She isn't an artist in the usual sense. She doesn't paint. She doesn't play a musical instrument. I've never known her to create any art objects, and public speaking is not her strong talent.

But when it comes to the gift of appreciating others, she is superbly blessed. Hers is not a gushy, uncritical appreciation, but one that is honest, perceptive, and trustworthy. And she expresses it not just through her words but with her face and her gestures.

People who can sincerely appreciate others have a unique gift. Like the woman who brought the ointment to Jesus, they affirm us as persons. They focus on our strengths, and in so doing help us deal with our weaknesses. They release something within us to reach for higher expression.

Like Jesus, we respond, "A beautiful thing has been done to us."

Prayer: So often, in moments of uncertainty about ourselves, O God, you affirm us through the expression of appreciation from a friend. Accept our thanks. Through Jesus our Lord. Amen.

Read Isaiah 41: 17–20.

SOMETHING FROM NOTHING

**I will open rivers on the bare heights.
Isaiah 41: 18.**

The God of the Old Testament is supposed to be a stern, bewhiskered disciplinarian who says "an eye for an eye, a tooth for a tooth." Justice is measured out carefully, one grain of sand for you, one for me.

But who is this God who keeps interrupting the nice Old Testament neatness and orderliness with comments like today's text? Listen: "When the poor seek water and there is none . . . I will open up rivers on the bare heights!" Not just a cupful for the parched tongue. A whole river! And not an old river, or a river rediscovered. Not an underground river bursting its way through to the surface. A new river! There was never a river there before. Only the bare heights. That is even more surprising. A river in the valley we can picture. Even an old river following a new course. But on the bare heights? What is this?

This is the gospel breaking through, beginning to show, asserting itself. Not just a revision or a recasting. NEW! Where there was nothing (in your life), now there is plenty. And where we knew a careful cautious God, there is now a reckless, unfettered God, who makes of a dark cross a door; of death, life. Of nothing, everything. Praise God!

Prayer: Forgive us our cautious, timid ways; you are ready to pour out new life on us. Amen.

Read Luke 12: 49–53.

WHAT DO YOU THINK I CAME FOR?

"Do you suppose that I came to bring peace to the world?"
Luke 12: 51 (T.E.V.).

I first remember hearing the word "paradox" at church, when the preacher said something about paradox in the sermon. To read that Jesus, the prince of peace, said he came to bring division has always been one of the big paradoxes for me. Jesus' statement seems contradictory. It's a hard saying. I think it must have been hard for Jesus to speak. Certainly, it's hard for me to hear or read.

Division, conflict, trouble—these are not what most of us want. We prefer peace. OUR kind of peace. Knowing what to expect during a worship service. Getting along well with friends. Living without tension in our families. Having only our own lives to look after. Finding decisions clear-cut and easy to make. Viewing the past with complacency and the future with comfort.

That's the kind of peace Jesus didn't bring. Jesus confronts us with tough choices. He came dividing people from people and stressing that the persons who are really related are those who share their faith in God, not those united by bonds of legal vows, similar genes, national pride, sex or age, race or income. He disturbs our contented existence by offering us the peace of following him.

Prayer: God, give us peace. Help us live it. Amen.

83

Read Daniel 9: 3–12.

COURAGE FOR THE ASKING

**Daniel . . . told them to seek mercy of the God of heaven concerning this mystery.
Daniel 2: 17–18.**

The saying, "There are no atheists in foxholes" implies that when we are in trouble we turn to God, and afterwards we forget him. Obviously, religious faith ought not to come to the surface only in an emergency. Isn't there something demeaning in the picture of frightened people on their knees begging God's mercy?

Not at all! Where else do you go in a time of danger? The book of Daniel was addressed to people whose heroes had carried out a successful rebellion, but who now wondered at the frightful retribution which might lie ahead. In such a situation Daniel counseled, "Get down on your knees." That's the answer for us too, when real trouble comes.

When I was in the hospital, preparing for open heart surgery, I prayed a lot. More often than I usually do! My chances were good, but if the surgeons thought of it as a routine operation I had a hard time seeing it that way. Looking back, I'm grateful for all that happened. How else would I have known how real God's help can be in a time of danger?

There are frightening things ahead in everyone's life. It is reassuring to know that when the time comes to jump into a foxhole, God will already be waiting there.

Prayer: O God, I remember many times when I needed you and you were very near. Thank you for your presence. Amen.

Read Luke 12: 6–7.

VALUED!

"You are of more value than many sparrows."
Luke 12: 7.

Many things can make us feel we have little value. Someone forgets your name. Someone gets more attention than
you. You're the one who doesn't get asked. Your birthday
is forgotten. You're criticized. If we let these things get to
us, we start to question our own worth. We can feel less
important than a sparrow hopping on the ground.

Jesus assures us that before God we are not forgotten:
we are special. Everything about us is remembered and
cherished. When we feel like sparrows, it's good to remember this.

One Christmas I was feeling low about myself. Everyone
seemed to be better than I was. I felt a failure and really
wondered whether to go on. On that Christmas Eve a special delivery package came. When I opened it, tears came
to my eyes. A friend had made me a notebook covered
with a collage. On it were my favorite things and things my
friend appreciated in me. As I look at the collage now, it
gives me a feeling of worth. I want to go on.

Think of several things about yourself that are valuable.
Write them down so that when you're feeling like a sparrow you can remember your importance before God. Do
the same for someone you appreciate and let them know.

Prayer: O Lord, when we feel worthless, remind us of our
value. Let us be your remembrance to others. Amen.

LIFTED

"Go and sit in the lowest place."
Luke 14: 10.

I know a man who has tried to be president of every organization he belongs to. He's developed the easy style of a professional conventioneer and invites everyone out to dinner. Underneath this exterior is a deep insecurity. He wants to be liked and feel important. Once he shared with me that his parents tried to make him feel small. This sharing made him more accessible and I liked him more than ever.

Often the way we try to exalt ourselves is a cover-up for insecurity. We try to put our best foot forward because we're afraid no one will like us if they see the other foot.

Jesus suggests that our efforts to build ourselves up will only bring us down. If we sit in the lowest place to begin with we can move up from there.

The lower places of humility and service—or of depression, fear, weakness, uncertainty—are hard to sit in because we've been taught to avoid or deny them. Perhaps if we acknowledge their reality, we will be lifted up.

What is the lowest place for you now? Go and sit there for awhile.

Prayer: O God, we are proud and want to be liked and accepted. Let us feel your acceptance lifting us from the lowest places. Amen.

Read Philippians 4: 4–13.

DETERMINATION

I am ready for anything through the strength of the one who lives within me.
Philippians 4: 13 (Phillips).

Living with rheumatoid arthritis has caused me to shift gears of thought many times. I found myself in a continuous state of overcoming and then falling again. "There must be a better way," I decided. The way? *Determination*!

I share my recipe for determination with the hope that it will help others who live with personal disappointment or suffering. (1) Begin anew each morning. Do not linger on yesterday's pain. (2) Thank God for the gift of each new day. Trust God for the outcome. (3) Seek medical guidance on amount of rest and exercise right for you, thereby preventing physical setbacks. (4) Keep planning for the future. This will keep your faith alive. (5) On days of extreme trouble or pain, reflect upon the many times God's love enables you to endure. (6) Reach out to another's need. Realize the full impact of God's love by sharing it! (7) Claim the strength of Christ within you—the secret for finding true determination to overcome pain and disappointments. This yields a faith-filled walk into the future. And Christ will be with you each step of the way!

Prayer: Thank you for being patient with us, Father. We see so clearly now that we were trying too hard on our own strength. Help us to persevere with the strength of Christ within us. Amen.

Read Exodus 4: 13–17.

FOR FRIENDS

"Is there not Aaron, your brother, the Levite?"
Exodus 4: 14.

Friend, I need you
When I can't speak.
I need your strength
When I am weak.

So many times I find myself
Alone, not knowing what to do.
I know you'd help, if you could see
How deeply I depend on you.

And in the joyous moments
When I would gladly share
Even then, to be fulfilled,
I need to have you there.

For you are my friend, even my brother.
We die inside without each other.

Prayer: Father, thank you for my friends. Thank you for bonds of human companionship and kinship which make life more whole. Thank you for your love which binds persons together and deepens relationships. Draw me closer to you, that I may be close to others. Amen.

FINDING MY PLACE

**Lord, thou hast been our dwelling place in all generations.
Psalm 90: 1.**

Do you feel almost unmade as yet? You want to feel born to people and a great cause. Perhaps you feel that something keeps you from the world that now is? If this is your mood you need to be awakened—today, to the fact that *already* you are a person. Your birth is in the past tense.

Remember that often the mind lags behind the act. At the end of a war, the truce already is declared before the last soldier lays down his arms. So the wish to be more a part of life may be the mind lagging back from the fact that your birth already has taken place. You *are* in life, and part of it!

Wishing for more of life may be reaching in the wrong direction for a gift that lies ready to be grasped and unwrapped. Wish in the right direction. Pray, conjure, and quest for what your life should be in the days and years ahead.

You are the key for God's unlocking imprisoned events and happenings that should take place through you. You are alive and with God's help and leading, you are ready to act!

Prayer: Lord, I thank you that I truly am alive; open my mind to see what needs to happen because I am here and ready to be directed. In Christ's name. Amen.

THE IMPLACABLE CHRIST

"When you leave, shake off the dust."
Mark 6: 11.

The young Christian earnestly advocated a service project in the community in faith that funds would materialize, although the regular budget of his church had been undersubscribed. The minister whispered to the finance chairman, "Placate him."

The young man's project came up annually but the Board always deferred it. Eventually, he was no longer seen in the sanctuary. He now sought to serve those of whose needs he was aware through channels outside his church.

Now this young man was such a winsome Christian. He remembered the change his father's conversion had made in their home. His caring could not be confined to a "practical" budget. And he was consistent to the point of giving you the shirt off his back although he had a family to provide for.

He left the church an uneasy question for them to live with. Unlike the rich young ruler, was this young man going sorrowfully away only to move *toward* his Master rather than away from him? Toward the same Master who upset things in the Temple and fed a multitude on a mountainside? Christ does not multiply loaves unless we first surrender them to him. He will not be pacified by shallow devotion or short-sighted vision.

Prayer: Lord God, give us faith to hear what you're saying to us and begin to do your will more surely today. Amen.

Read Luke 12: 22–31.

STOP ALONG THE WAY

"Consider the lilies, how they grow; they neither toil nor spin; yet I tell you, even Solomon in all his glory was not arrayed like one of these."
Luke 12: 27.

It used to require six months to cross the American continent by covered wagon. Now we can jet across in less than six hours. (Someday we may reduce the traveling time to six minutes!) Since "being there" seems to have become the most important thing, the less time we can spend "getting there" the better off we think we will be.

Yet I often find myself dissatisfied even though I have arrived where I intended to be. I feel in some vague and uneasy way that I have missed something, and that "something," I suspect, was along the way. I had become so intent on being there that I did not pay much attention to what happened around me as I went.

Jesus bids us consider the lilies of the field, fragile things along the path, which may be alive only for today. Yet in their brief moment of glory they tell us more of the providence of God than Solomon in all his years of material splendor. Those things along the path, which we tend to rush past, may hold the meaning of life. Our Lord sometimes calls us away from the pursuit of our earnest intentions to behold a less-noticed beauty. He bids us stop, occasionally, along our journey, in order to perceive the evidence of God's care.

Prayer: O God, let us never be so intent on "being there" that we fail to perceive your glory along the path. Amen.

Read Genesis 41: 14-16, 33-36.

THE LONG PULL

Joseph . . . entered the service of Pharaoh king of Egypt.
Genesis 41: 46.
I do not box as one beating the air.
1 Corinthians 9: 26.

There are times when we seem to be stripped of every hope—battered and beaten down. In such times the soul sinks into despair or rises to nobler heights. For Joseph it was the latter. Thirteen years of his life had been spent in slavery—seven of them in the king's prison. Yet Joseph settled down for the long pull and came through as a stronger character, courageous and resolute.

We know that God was with him, but what did Joseph do to remain strong?

First, Joseph busied himself. He didn't become embittered, sit and mope, bewail his lot, pity himself. He got busy adjusting to prison routine.

Second, Joseph lost himself in concern for others. Witness his interest in the baker and the butler.

Third, Joseph was alert to know and grow. When he finally appeared before Pharaoh, he was at ease in court life, fluent in politics, government, etc. He had rubbed not just his elbows but his mind with the king's own imprisoned, and he turned a dungeon into a university, as it were, with a political science as his major.

Beyond all the above, you and I have one advantage over Joseph. If we take even halting steps toward Jesus, we can depend on him to help us come out right!

Prayer: Our Father, when we are down, help us to get up and keep going. Through Christ, who keeps us going. Amen.

92

Read Genesis 45: 4-13.

GOD'S UNSEARCHABLE WAYS

"So it was not you who sent me here, but God."
Genesis 45: 8.
In everything God works for good with those who love him.
Romans 8: 28.

The world looking upon Joseph, on his way to slavery in Egypt "wouldn't have given a nickel for his chances." To all appearances it was the end. But it really was only the beginning. Joseph, looking back, explained it all as God's "doings."

How many times has God's providence been real to you? Perhaps you have escaped "by a hair" or survived by a "miracle." But other times when your hands of flesh have beaten against doors of iron that would not yield, you have cried out, "Why? Why?"

The unsearchable providence of God is as old as humankind. Job wrestled with it, "searching to find God out." We too find ourselves baffled. We cannot know, we cannot understand. We can only say, "Our Father." We can only be confident that back of all that is happening we are being kept by God's love, and that "all things work together for good . . . ." (Rom. 8: 28, K.J.V.)

Life is like the weaving of a great tapestry, with the weavers, each busy at a little task, not knowing much about the whole. But the *master weaver*, in spite of the flaws, is perfecting the grand design. There's a power that shapes our ends, weave them how we will.

Prayer: Heavenly Father, give us faith to believe that your purpose of love is unfolding itself in our lives and in the happenings of our time. Amen.

Read Leviticus 16: 29-34.

THE IMPORTANCE OF REPENTANCE

"For on this day shall atonement be made for you, to cleanse you; from all your sins you shall be clean before the LORD." Leviticus 16: 30.

He paused outside the door to his son's room. He fumbled with the change in his pocket and picked at his collar. He swayed a bit awkwardly from side to side. How often it had been the boy's turn to say the words. It seemed easy then, just listening. Why couldn't it be that way now! But no. He knew better. Finally he took hold of the doorknob and eased open the door. His throat came unstuck. The words tumbled out. "Bob, I'm really sorry about last night. I . . . I got upset and I said too much."

Bob looked startled. He had just gotten out of bed. He hesitated for a moment, then answered, "I understand, Dad. Thanks." For five long seconds the two just stared at each other. Suddenly the boy broke into a grin. The man nodded, gave a quick sigh of relief, and then bounded downstairs to breakfast.

Sometimes repentance is the only way to restore a closeness we yearn for. In ancient Israel, the people every year performed a complex ritual to cleanse themselves of sin. It was the only way to clear the pathways to the living God. For us it is simpler now, but tougher too. It's not ritual. It's face to face. It's "Darling, I'm sorry." "Frank, I was wrong." "O God, forgive!" Sometimes it's the only way back.

Prayer: Help me repent whenever I need to! Amen.

Read Micah 7: 1-7.

WHAT'S A SAVIOR?

But I will look for the LORD,
I will wait for God my saviour; my God will hear me.
Micah 7: 7 (N.E.B.).

What's a savior?

The word means "the one who makes sound," or "keeps sound." Or it may mean "the one who heals or makes whole." Or, more important in the book of Micah, "the one who delivers from oppression."

Jesus our Savior came not for a certain group in a certain place at a certain time; nor was his work limited to one nation, one race, one culture; nor was it to save us from this world for the next. His work was to set right what was wrong in human life—in all human life. He didn't come to save us out of this evil world, but to equip us to live in it with lives open to God's grace and our neighbor's need.

To know Jesus as savior is to know through him that you are loved by God; that there is nothing you can do to win that love, to earn it, or to destroy it. Whenever people begin to know that love and to live in it, they know Christ as savior—the one who makes things right and whole and sound. "To you is born . . . a Savior, who is Christ the Lord." (Luke 2: 11)

Prayer: Jesus, Savior, you have come into our world to deliver us from our darkness. By the power of your love keep us sound in your light and righteousness and make us whole. Amen.

BRIDGING THE GAP

**In these last days he has spoken to us by a Son.
Hebrews 1: 2.**

"Oh! *Mother!* Weren't *you* ever young?"

The least effective reply in the world to that remark begins with, "Why when *I* was your age . . ." Youths don't really believe that parents ever were their age.

If a communication gap can develop between child and parent, how much greater the possibility for a communication gap between us humans and God. How difficult it is for the created to believe that the creator really understands our trials and tribulations. How easy it is to say, "God, if you expect me to be calm in all *this* confusion, you just don't understand the situation!"

Christmas assures us that God *does* understand the situation—*our* situation. The incarnation is the story of God walking in *our* shoes. For thirty-three years Jesus walked the same paths we walk. When we talk to God about the perils of the trail, God knows from experience what we're talking about. We read, "For we have not a high priest who is unable to sympathize with our weaknesses, but one who in every respect has been tempted as we are, yet without sin." (Heb. 4: 15)

Prayer: Thank you, Father, for speaking to me through your son. Thank you for telling me through him that you understand the problems of my world. I see it now: in him you experienced the problems I experience. Thank you! Amen.

Read Philippians 4: 10-20.

FACING ECONOMIC CHANGES

I can do all things in him who strengthens me.
Philippians 4: 13.

Recently our congressman paid a much publicized visit to our county in order, as he put it, "not to speak, but to listen." He wanted to know what his constituents were thinking. The subject most often raised by the overflow crowds was the economic situation—jobs and inflation.

Many of the economic changes we must face are difficult and depressing: a person who cannot find a job, a household facing rising food costs, an older person threatened by the shrinking value of his or her Social Security check. Whatever form an economic change may take, we must deal with the change somehow.

Paul, who wrote the beautiful words in today's Scripture, clearly lived in economic insecurity. How did he cope? The Good News Bible translated verses 12-13: "I know what it is to be in need and what it is to have more than enough. I have learned this secret, so that anywhere, at any time, I am content, whether I am full or hungry, whether I have too much or too little. I have the strength to face all conditions by the power that Christ gives me." Christ can give us the power to face any change!

Prayer: Jesus, you worked as a Galilean carpenter and faced economic change. Be with us as we face future change. Amen.

Read Isaiah 40: 25-31.

MAKING CHANGES

**They who wait for the LORD shall renew their strength,
they shall mount up with wings like eagles.
Isaiah 40: 31.**

Sometimes we have "spiritual brownouts"—times when our spiritual and emotional lives burn low, when we continue to function only by a hard, cold heave of the will. When this happens, we *need* change in our lives; we need to tap more power. Such change must be initiated by us, no one can do it for us. It may be to schedule an extra fifteen minutes each day to talk with God, it may be an afternoon off, or a long look at our priorities. Whatever the answer to our need, we should remember that God created us, God understands us.

Today's Scripture probes both the depth of God's understanding of us and the heights of God's power to help us. God knows us intimately, knows our limitations, knows our problems, knows the nitty-gritty little things in life that wear us down. But God doesn't just say "I understand." Surely Isaiah is picturing here much more than a God of sympathy—here is a God of power! Power like the eagles, soaring into the heavens! That is the kind of God we worship, and when we change our lives to become more open to God, that is the kind of power we tap.

Prayer: O God of love and power, make us aware that some of the needed changes in our lives must be brought about by us. In the name of your Son. Amen.

Read Psalm 19: 1–6.

THE UNIVERSE

**The heavens are telling the glory of God;
and the firmament proclaims his handiwork.
Psalm 19: 1.**

The evening filled up quickly with summer sounds; freshened by a night breeze, it invited participation in the world outside my home. I stepped into a path that could lead, I reminded myself, to any place on planet earth. But more immediately, it led through a wooded area and sloped upward to yield a view of the Ohio River.

Then suddenly the evening filled up with stars. At the edge of the trees, the night horizon climbed into the sky. An up-curving world fused into a field of bright stars. I stood corrected by the Voice of the Universe: my path could lead *beyond planet earth* to anywhere in the starry space above me! Even if my feet would never explore that space, my eyes now relayed its beauty.

In that moment my mind broke out of its earthly boundaries and responded to the infinite message of creation. As if with the shepherds of old, I listened to the "song of stars" and heard in their symphony servants giving God glory.

Prayer: Our Father, in a universe so tuned to your glory, may we be in tune with your power and harmony. By your Spirit move us today beyond familiar horizons to a larger life. In Jesus' name we pray. Amen.

Read Acts 10: 34–43.

BEYOND THE BARRIERS

"The truth I have now come to realise," he said, "is that God does not have favourites, but that anybody of any nationality who fears God and does what is right is acceptable to him." Acts 10: 34–35 (The Jerusalem Bible).

It is trite, but true. Eleven o'clock on Sunday morning remains the most segregated hour in our national life.

Few of us are part of truly integrated congregations. More often, we live and work side by side with people of different races, but worship in different churches.

Today is Martin Luther King, Jr.'s birthday. Remembering Dr. King, we can again hear the cadences of his "I Have a Dream" speech, challenging us toward a world where all God's children are affirmed and accepted.

Can we speak of unity in the church and ignore the fact that the color of our skin still largely determines which of our brothers and sisters in Christ we shall and shall not worship with? Haven't we, on occasion, been guilty of keeping peace in the church at the price of our integrity?

"God does not have favourites," said Peter after his encounter with Cornelius. Human boundaries and distinctions that divide and hurt God's children are enemies of the gospel.

As with Peter, the lesson is not easy and may be painful. Yet the challenge remains. To seek unity is to seek to destroy those things which separate us.

What are you doing to make God's vision a reality?

Prayer: Forgive our divisions, Lord. Help us today, even in small ways, to mirror your all-inclusive love. Amen.

Read Romans 8: 38–39.

ANGUISH

For I am sure that . . . [nothing] will be able to separate us from the love of God in Christ Jesus our Lord. Romans 8: 38–39.

After graduating from high school as a distinguished student, our youngest began to be disoriented and confused. He and a group of his friends had begun, as did millions of our nation's youth, to use marihuana and other street drugs. Our son was one of those who could not cope with the effects. Things went from bad to worse as pot smoking became the means of trying to shut out the downward plunge of his self-esteem. My husband and I were depressed and disappointed for our bright, studious youngster, but we soon learned to share our burden with friends. This, combined with insight given by professionals, helped us to acquire a more balanced perspective.

Our son failed at everything he tried and became lost and withdrawn. After we had tried many avenues of help—psychiatry, our city's drug abuse program, the Mental Health facilities—it became clear that he was mentally and emotionally disturbed. We had him committed to the hospital by way of the courts.

Prayer: Dear Father, only you can give meaning to sadness. Sometimes we can only cast all our cares upon you. Help us today to give to you our every sadness, disappointment, fear, or confusion. Thank you for the reality of your leading and your love. Amen.

Read Matthew 5: 14–16.

HOW ARE YOU DOING, PREACHER?

"Let your light so shine before men, that they may see your good works and give glory to your Father who is in heaven." Matthew 5: 16.

Every person is busy preaching some kind of sermon to the people around. (Understand a sermon as "an organized presentation of the gospel." Then realize there are a variety of ways to "present" the sermon.)

We usually think most sermons are presented on Sundays by the minister of the church. But, in truth, every day, each of us conveys some kind of message about the significance of the Christian gospel. The way we live is a vivid presentation of what we believe about Christ and his word.

What are *you* saying?

Is your sermon in focus and clear, or do you communicate chaos and confusion? Does your life speak boldly of Christ or is it an embarrassed apology for your faith? Do you reflect a caring God who values all people the same? Do you speak convincingly of forgiveness and mercy? Do you reflect spiritual growth and progress?

Every Christian a preacher
every life a sermon!
Well, preacher, how are you doing?

Prayer: Lord, help me to be careful with my daily living. When people see me and what I do, I want them to say only the best about you. For Christ's sake. Amen.

Read John 1: 43–49.

THANK GOD FOR PURPLE HOUSES!

Nathanael said to him, "Can anything good come out of Nazareth?" Philip said to him, "Come and see."
John 1: 46.

I passed an odd building in a neighboring community a while back. It was a house, freshly painted. What caught my eye was the color. It was a stark purple.

Something in me wanted to stop, get out, and paint the building white.

A silly reaction, I admit. But houses are not supposed to be purple or black or bright orange. They are supposed to be painted white or brown or yellow.

"Nothing good ever comes out of Nazareth." Fortunately for Nathanael, he did not let his ignorant opinion keep him from meeting the man who would forever change his life.

How about us? Do we have our minds so made up about people and issues that we miss a lot that they have to offer? Do we "write off" everyone who is in some way different from us?

Have we reduced every ethnic, religious, or social group to a stereotype?

God in his wisdom has created a world with variety and surprise. It is a gift from him in which we should take great delight.

Prayer: Father, thank you for purple houses and different kinds of people. Help us to appreciate variety in others. Amen.

Read Romans 12: 3–8.

THE QUILT MAKER

For as in one body we have many members, and all the members do not have the same function, so we, though many, are one body in Christ, and individually members one of another. Romans 12: 4–5.

Her wrinkled hands busily pushing a needle in and out, the white-haired lady sat at the arts and crafts fair making a coverlet. Behind her, arranged in a colorful display, were quilts. "Patchwork." "Wedding Ring." "Crazy Quilt." "Log Cabin." Each had a name and each was put together, piece by piece, into a beautiful, intricate pattern. In "piecing her quilts," the woman took many scraps of cloth and created a coverlet that would delight the eyes with beauty and warm the body on a cold winter night.

People. White. Black. Young. Old. Men. Women. Poets. Factory workers. Teachers. Farmers. Ministers. Truck drivers. Each life of different material, some smooth and elegant as velvet; some rough and plain as burlap. Still others, soft and warm as wool. Dull lives. Exciting lives. Frantic lives. Calm lives. Each is a piece of living in the design of God's world. Each is a scrap until in Christ we come together. Then we become a creation that is beautiful and warming to the world's soul.

Patchwork becomes a holy pattern.

Prayer: Dear Lord, thank you that we may be different and yet may still belong to you and to each other. Accept our piece of life and pattern it in your design. Today, teach us to recognize the beauty and wisdom shown to us by your handiwork. Amen.

Read 1 Corinthians 15: 12–20.

HOW CAN WE BE SURE?

But in fact Christ has been raised from the dead, the first fruits of those who have fallen asleep.
1 Corinthians 15: 20.

A question deep in our minds is, "How can we be sure there is anything beyond the grave except dark nothingness, non-existence?" Job, the ancient seer, asked the question of all humankind, " 'If a man die, shall he live again?' " (Job 14: 14)

People have always sought some kind of proof for life beyond death. For example, in recent writings we find descriptions of those who were pronounced medically dead, but who "came back" and described their experiences of the life beyond. Then, too, many believe that life here does not really make sense unless there is a future life. For them, as someone said, "One world at a time is the shallowest motto by which we may live."

All these thoughts are interesting and valuable. But Christians base their faith on the two most significant truths they know. One is the love of God. We know we can commit our loved ones and ourselves to our Father's care.

Our other great truth is the resurrection of Christ. As Paul said, "If Christ has not been raised, your faith is futile . . . But in fact Christ has been raised from the dead." (1 Cor. 15: 17, 20)

Prayer: Lord, you have given us faith to trust our lives and those dear to us to your love. Strengthen us to think of death with quiet confidence, knowing that with you, life is eternal. Amen.

Read John 3: 8.

TO CREATE

In the beginning God created the heavens and the earth. The earth was without form and void, and darkness was upon the face of the deep; and the Spirit of God was moving.
Genesis 1: 1, 2.

I experience periods of void and darkness in my life. Listen as a wondrous force infiltrates me. Envision the power of God at work. As in the beginning, as in the now . . . there is the Wind of Creation . . . .

> I stand barefoot on white gypsum dunes,
> and enjoy the moist coolness beneath the dry
> surface heat. I gaze at majestic mountains
> penetrating cloud swirled skies. I hear the wind
> speak of change, and know this wide desert horizon
> to be but one bit of creation; for the mountains
> are being moved, refined and etched by the elements;
> the gypsum covers old paths, and skies display
> designs for dreamers. In cross currents,
> sudden drafts, and turbulent storms, the
> unpredictable wind prevails. Therefore mountain
> slopes become grains of sand, the dunes travel on,
> and skies show forth glory.

Prayer Thoughts: Mysteriously God gives the Holy Spirit to prevail in my life. I will yield and be filled with this cleansing, refreshing, and invigorating gift of God. I rejoice and give all praise and thanks to God, asking God to move in me today. Amen.

EXTRA LEGAL

**But if you are led by the Spirit you are not under the law.
Galatians 5: 18.**

O to be outside, out from under, out of reach of the law! Then I could do just as I liked without fear of anyone stopping me! That would be freedom.

Surely, at some time you have been tempted to entertain such a wish. But a friend once remarked that the law is meant to protect me from myself. The law is a constant reminder that I must not act in ways which in others I would be quick to condemn. Paul speaks of these acts of wickedness as being works of the flesh. Laws are designed to discourage, prohibit, punish such conduct.

It is when self takes the bit in its teeth and charges off unchecked that the terrors of chaos ensue. This is no freedom. This is anarchy or worse.

But let the self become subject to the Spirit, and the law becomes as useless as a stepladder to a honey bee. "But the fruit of the Spirit is love, joy, peace, patience, kindness, goodness, faithfulness, gentleness, self-control; against such there is no law." (Gal. 5: 22, 23)

Our trouble is that often when we think self has been subjugated to the Spirit we deceive ourselves. There are segments of our mind and throbs of our heart and sub-conscious passions that revolt and still need the commandments and discipline of the law. Until the self becomes subject to the Spirit the law is an aid to freedom.

Prayer: Father, conquer the enemy within and make us free. Amen.

Read Psalm 108: 1–5.

A QUALITY OF CELEBRATION

I will sing and make melody!
    Awake, my soul!
Psalm 108: 1.

I am still overwhelmed at all the riches that have come my way simply because I held out open hands. I own forgiveness, love, freedom, grace, direction, and much, much more.

MORNING IS CERTAINLY DIFFERENT NOW, ISN'T IT?

Really! Now there's a happy sense of expectancy to the day. With a charted course to follow, life takes on a quality of celebration. I want to tell you about it with a poem, Lord, if that's okay.

AHA! A GLIMMER OF THE COURAGE TO CREATE.

> Joy dances out my ears
> Laughter out my eyes
> Content delights my fingertips
> And happy struggles through my toes
> Breath explodes to taste the day
> A body leaping out all free
> Who is that blooming down the path?
> Lord Jesus Christ, it's ME!
> Yes, late and finally, life, it's me.

WELCOME, CHILD, WELCOME.

Prayer: Thanks for inviting me to your party, God. I'm having a great time. Amen.

Read Isaiah 59: 9–15.

CRYING IN THE DARK

We look for light, and behold, darkness,
  and for brightness, but we walk in gloom.
Isaiah 59: 9.

Look, here is a picture album. On the first page appears the title: *Our Baby's First Years.* Page two displays the picture taken through the nursery window. There is Baby, round, squint-eyed, and beautiful!

Next comes Baby in Mommy's arms, Baby on Daddy's shoulders, Baby with the first toys, Baby in a bright new stroller. See Baby's first birthday picture! Blow out one candle, Baby. Blow out your life. For the rest of the album is empty. Who sees the X-rays the hospital took of Baby when Mommy came to the emergency room last night? Who reads the police report the next day? Who knows why Baby cried too much, ate too much, wet too much? Who was aware of Mommy's tears? of Daddy's pain? of Grandma's anger? of Uncle's "problems"?

We look for light, but find darkness. God's world is not all bright and shining. The animals destroy each other for food; the balance of plants and moisture has gone wrong; the mist has long since ceased to water the garden. Truth is lacking. Where has it gone? Where has gone the goodness? the light? Where is God's image?

"God saw it, and it displeased him." Can we see it, too? In this Year of the Child, how can we restore light to a child's dark world? A child cries. Do we hear?

Prayer: Someone's crying, God. Come by here!

Read Job 38: 1–3, 19–38.

DIVINE PERSPECTIVE OF SUFFERING

"Naked I came from my mother's womb, and naked shall I return; the LORD gave, and the LORD has taken away; blessed be the name of the LORD."
Job 1: 21.

Carol died the same day as Hubert Humphrey—of the same disease. She was much younger, a teacher who loved her students, a person who gave much to life. But through her illness she came to know God's love with deep trust.

Her parents suffered more than Carol. She was their only child. Finally, when hospital therapy could help no more, they took her home to spend her last Christmas, where each day together grew more precious. Through their suffering, their love and trust in God triumphed.

Mrs. Cox wrote afterward, "Carol's birth, life, death, and eternal life have been and always will be to us God's miracle. She gave so much to us that our hearts will be forever thankful."

That quiet shout of praise to God has to remind us of Job, who out of his deep anguish was able to whisper, "Blessed be the name of the Lord."

Now, how did they manage that? Job and Carol's parents? How did they cause their worst defeat to be swallowed up in victory? By trusting God completely. God made it possible for them to praise. Praising God through our blackest night is a lesson known automatically by the stars. We humans have to learn it experience by experience.

Prayer: Strengthen us, O God, to praise you in our Gethsemane.

Read Psalm 25: 1–5.

THE UNKNOWN PATH

He leads me in paths of righteousness
for his name's sake.
Psalm 23: 3.

Divorce is not the path I have chosen! This can't possibly be the Lord's will for me!

For those who walk it, the path of righteousness is not a stroll, it is a journey. We are being led. Sometimes we do not choose to follow. The path leads beside still water, but sometimes we do not drink. There are green pastures, but we refuse the rest they offer. We are being led—not pushed. We cannot run out ahead, attempting somehow to take the lead ourselves or to catch a glimpse of what lies around that uncertain corner.

One thing is sure—we go forth not knowing. To go forth not knowing is the essence of faith. It is not an easy way. The demands of righteousness are met only by faith. Faith must shine brightest when the way is the darkest and when there is no answer to the call we make except the echo of our own voices. Can divorce possibly be a path of righteousness? Yes! Any path that leads to growth, any path that requires faith, can be a path of righteousness.

Prayer: Show us the path again, Father, for we seem to have lost our way. We are confused. Teach us to recognize the end in the beginning—the beginning in the end. We are weak, Father. Show us your strength in our weakness. We have made promises we failed to keep. Help us to believe in *your* promises. Amen.

Read 1 Samuel 3: 2–10.

A BIT LIKE GRANDPA

[Samuel] ran to Eli, and said, "Here I am, for you called me."
1 Samuel 3: 5.

One morning when Rosemary was about four years old, we went in to find her lying thoughtfully in bed. "God spoke to me last night," she said, "and, you know, God sounded a bit like Grandpa." Grandpa was very flattered when he heard that story!

It should not be surprising, though, that the voice of God in our hearts should have a familiar accent. God's voice will most readily come in the tones of those we love and who love us. Rosemary thought God sounded a bit like Grandpa, and Samuel thought God spoke like Eli, and nothing could be more natural. God most easily speaks in our hearts like a person we know very, very well, and who cares for us greatly.

Turn that around for a moment and realize that you also speak to people. Will they ever hear the voice of God and think God sounds like you?

Prayer: Dear Lord, help us to hear your voice in the speech of people around us, especially those who love us. Help us also to think carefully before we speak so that your living word may stretch out through our words. May our accents be the accents of a love that cares, for the sake of Jesus Christ our Lord. Amen.

Read Psalm 72.

AMEN AND AMEN

Blessed be his glorious name for ever;
may his glory fill the whole earth!
Amen and Amen.
Psalm 72: 19.

When Bruce was only two and we would say grace at mealtimes, the only word he really knew was "Amen." With the rest of the family he would shut his eyes and mouth some words in holy style. On hearing "Amen" he would repeat it with gusto, pick up his spoon, and get on with the job of eating.

Now that is just how it should be. Say "Amen," and get on with the job. "May his glory fill the whole earth! Amen and Amen." Amen is the end of the prayer, but the beginning of the action. You must now go out and push the world a little nearer to that great hope. You pray for other people, then do something to help them. You confess your sins, then do what you can to set right your wrong. You give thanks to God, then enjoy what God has given. You praise God, then praise God with your life as well. Your prayers are a blueprint for your life. God will use you to make your prayers come true.

Bruce knows what to do after saying "Amen." Do you?

Prayer: Lord God, I hardly dare pray anything for fear of what it means for my life. Help me not to be afraid of prayer but to see that through my prayers you can use me better in your service for the sake of Jesus Christ our Lord. Amen.

Read Psalm 95: 1–7.

A NEW DAY

Let us come into his [God's] presence with thanksgiving. Psalm 95: 2.

"I begin each day giving thanks to God for what I can still do," remarked a friend trying to adjust to the fact that she has Parkinson's disease. I had asked how her illness was affecting her attitude toward life. "I feel pretty depressed sometimes, but people have really helped a lot," she added. Her husband and young children have accepted additional household responsibilities, and a weekly Bible study and prayer group have provided much support.

Frequently we attempt to face adversity by hoping for better days to come. "The sun will come up tomorrow" sings Annie in the popular Broadway musical. It can be helpful and often essential to recognize that feelings and situations do change. Tomorrow *is* a new day. It is equally important, however, to live in the *present,* not the future. *Today* is also a new day.

Can we make a new attempt to begin each day conscious that we are living every moment in the presence of God? *Today* we are surrounded by God's great love for us. *Today* we have the opportunity to do what we can. Thank God for *this* new day!

Prayer: Eternal God, we honor you as the Lord of yesterday, today, and tomorrow. Help us to live today knowing that we are embraced by your love and care. This new day is a precious gift and we give you thanks for it, through Jesus Christ our Lord, Amen.

Read Genesis 29: 15–27.

THE DETOURS OF TROUBLED LOVE

So Jacob worked seven years for Rachel, and they seemed like a few days because he loved her.
Genesis 29: 20 (N.E.B.).

Lovers are notorious for their impatience. It is unbelievable that Jacob would be willing to work seven years for Rachel, much less fourteen. What a long detour! And what a waste! Jacob would have had every right to be impatient.

How essential it is to learn patience, as we struggle along some of the detours of troubled love! Recovering from the shattering of a romance, making the most of an imperfect marriage, are experiences which remind us that pain is involved in loving. But even if we are hurt, we can't stop loving, or life shrivels. Therefore, we remain vulnerable.

"Love is very patient," Paul said, not meaning that love and patience go naturally together, but that love gives the power to acquire that almost impossible virtue. Most of us are not patient. We pray, "Give me patience, O Lord, but please hurry!" But some circumstances and relationships cannot be changed at all, and others are worked out only with painful slowness. The story of Jacob reminds us that there are some things which are so important that they are worth learning to be patient about.

Prayer: O God, when our patience runs out, and we protest the pain of our imperfect relationships, we give thanks for your patience with us and for your never-failing love. Amen.

115

Read Mark 6: 30-34.

ON GETTING INVOLVED

And he [Jesus] said to them, "Come away by yourselves to a lonely place, and rest a while." For many were coming and going, and they had no leisure even to eat.
Mark 6: 30–31.

Probably one of the most apt expressions for modern life is the one which characterizes great masses of people engaging in endless rounds of "frenetic activity." Interests outside our normal line of work do have a way of siphoning off our available time to the point where we find it difficult to sit down for a bite to eat!

And for what? To what detriment to our physical and emotional well-being do we take on yet another task while friends wonder how we do it and our loved ones silently hope we someday learn to say no.

There are important tasks which must be done. Perhaps there are those which only we can do. But there comes a point at which we can neither do our best for all our commitments nor maintain even a semblance of order in our lives. In short, there is a time when "getting involved" may *not* be the thing to do, and may well be the worst thing to do.

So we must decide, on our own scale of values, what are the most important things for us to do and then allow ample time for re-creation. All of us need time off. The wise person realizes this and doesn't become over involved—not even in "worthy" causes.

Prayer: Eternal God, your purposes are working themselves out even as I rest. Help me to pace myself so that I may glorify you when I am involved. In Christ. Amen.

Read Psalm 56.

GOD HEARS AND KNOWS

**Thou hast kept count of my tossings;
   put thou my tears in thy bottle!
   Are they not in thy book?
Psalm 56: 8.**

Last night was one of those times when, try as hard as I could, I simply could not get to sleep. It seemed to take all night to get an ounce of rest. Maybe my day was just too busy! Maybe it was the fact that one of my closest friends in the parish had gone from the Church Militant to the Church Triumphant. Maybe I had the grief and sorrow of the family so deep in my consciousness that all efforts to fall asleep, peacefully asleep, were doomed to failure from the start. Whatever the cause, I know it was not a restful night.

The psalmist knew what it was like to toss and turn and fail to get rest. He was haunted and hunted just as we are haunted and hunted by various important and not-so-important concerns. Our concerns sometimes weigh so heavily upon us that we are close to tears. At times we break down completely. At those times it is good to remember that lament and plea of the psalmist to God: ''Put thou my tears in thy bottle!''

God hears our cries so deeply that not even one tear can be lost! God hears and knows our deepest sighs and our deepest needs. Nothing that comes before God is lost!

Prayer: God, sometimes we hurt so badly that we think even you cannot hear us. Remind us of your Son who also shed tears and was comforted. In his name. Amen.

Read Song of Solomon 2: 1–13.

GOD'S PLAN

O LORD, how manifold are thy works!
  In wisdom hast thou made them all;
  the earth is full of thy creatures.
Psalm 104: 24.

Give me the woodland call, its earthy breeze,
Spare me the noise of every human-made thing;
Give me the shelter of great wide-branched trees,
With time to stop and hear the freshet sing.
Give me old fences not too high to climb
And laurel-covered mountains, high and steep,
Where rocks and gorges tell of tide and time,
Where eyes of night their endless vigil keep.
But let there be a bridge for my return
To make my daily bread and share as much
With comrades, as we live and love and learn.
United in a common, human touch.
These earthy things are part of God's great plan,
I capture them and hold them if I can.

Prayer: Eternal God, we thank you for the beauty of the earth. We know you give us promise with the budding and flowering of spring, the summer gardens, lush with food for our needs, the flaming leaves and ripened grain of harvest time, and the snow-covered mountain peaks and challenges of winter. We make our prayer with grateful hearts for all these gifts. Amen.

Read Mark 4: 35–41.

JESUS, DON'T YOU CARE?

Jesus stood up and commanded the wind, "Be quiet!" and he said to the waves, "Be still!" . . . there was a great calm.
Mark 4: 39 (T.E.V.).

If you are in a small boat, with a strong wind blowing and waves splashing menacingly over the sides, Good News would surely be that the shore is ten feet away—or that the storm will be over in five minutes. Jesus was supposed to be Good News. The disciples were in a boat, far from shore, and there was a terrible storm. They were really frightened. What was Jesus doing? Sleeping! "Jesus! Don't you care that we are about to die?" They couldn't understand how he could be so calm.

Jesus spoke and things happened immediately. The waves and the wind subsided. Then came the question that really must have stabbed: "How come you are frightened? Have you no faith?"

Do we get afraid or upset when the storm is raging—when everything is going wrong, or when we're swamped with work or worry? Does it seem as if God really doesn't care?

Was Jesus really saying to the disciples, "Trust me"? Is that what he is saying to you and me, today?

Lord, sometimes we are so worried and upset about things around us that all we can do is cry out. Help us for once to pause, and to pray, "Lord, help me to trust you more, and to believe that you really do care about what happens to me today." Amen.

Read Mark 7: 14–20.

IT'S AN INSIDE JOB!

**"From the inside, from a person's heart, come the evil ideas."
Mark 7: 21 (T.E.V.).**

Our Lord had come across the lake. The news spread quickly about what he did and said. Some Pharisees and teachers had come to see and listen. They couldn't remain silent any longer. Look at his followers and the way they eat! They are not doing it properly. Their hands haven't been cleaned properly; neither was the food prepared properly. They are breaking tradition and breaking the law.

Jesus quickly replies. He accuses them of hypocrisy. They distort and misinterpret the word of God. Besides all that, Jesus says, it's not what goes into a person that makes one unclean, but rather, what comes from within, from the heart.

Are we ever like those Pharisees? Do we judge sometimes by externals or rigidly interpret the rules, or fail to try to understand others? Are we ever, to some people, bad news, not good? Are we too legalistic in our approach to Christian living instead of emphasizing a person's relationship to Christ?

Sometimes, Lord, we attach much importance to appearances. Before we look at anyone else, though, please give us the courage and help we need to look inside at ourselves. Bring us the Good News, and help us to share it with those around us. Amen.

Read Mark 8: 27–30; Matthew 16: 13–20.

WHO AM I?

**"Who do you say I am?" Peter answered, "You are the Messiah."
Mark 8: 29 (T.E.V.).**

Caesarea Philippi. Would they ever forget it? What a question! "What are people saying about me?"

The answer was easy, because they had heard all kinds of comments about Jesus. Then he asked what *they* believed about him! That was putting it on the line. Peter was ready though. He said it all. "You are the Messiah, the Son of the living God."

What would I have said had he asked me? I would have been on the spot for sure! Messiah? The sent one from God? The fulfillment of Old Testament prophecy? Would I go that far? I wonder. What would my answer be to the most important question I could ever be asked? My faith is on the line. My life, too.

What about today? Are we not all asked the same question? I can put it off no longer. I have always said that the time wasn't quite right or that it wasn't quite convenient. I'm running out of excuses now. The question is still there, this time for me to answer. Christ is waiting. It's my turn! There is no one in front of me. It's my turn to answer.

Lord, the Good News is that you love me. Thank you. Even when I am slow to catch on, please don't give up on me. Amen.

Read Matthew 27: 1–22.

THE WORD OF DENIAL

Pilate said to them, "Then what shall I do with Jesus who is called Christ?" They all said, "Let him be crucified."
Matthew 27: 22.

This is the Word of Denial. Cruel and final words.

We are not so cruel. But often we would like to get rid of him. He is too good for us. His values play havoc with ours. He is not for our world. His "stuff" won't work. Kindness, love, forgiveness, patience, tenderness, meekness—is this good stock in trade for everyday life?

They got rid of Jesus, or thought they had, by crucifixion.

But we are more subtle. We would not hurt him. We would only ignore him. In the world of social and economic intercourse we give him no place. At the same time we give him lip service. We embalm him in poetry, bury him in sentiment, paint pictures of him, write and sing hymns to him, imprison him in ritual, cover him in worship, confine him to one day or hour, pray to him, praise him. We keep him out of the halls of education, the markets of trade, the arena of human relations, or the offices of professional life.

Strange twist of human nature. We need him and worship him, but how difficult it is to live by his way!

O God, make me aware of the subtleties of my nature by which I deny Jesus. Help me to open all the doors of my life to him, especially the ones which are so tightly locked. Amen.

Read Psalm 63.

THE SHADOW OF WINGS

For thou hast been my help,
  and in the shadow of thy wings I sing for joy.
Psalm 63: 7.

One bright spring morning I looked outside the study window. The sun made a sharp shadow as it hit the corner of the church. There was plenty of shade, and in that shade a flock of grosbeaks rummaged for food. I watched the pretty yellow, white, black, and gray birds feed right up to the bright edge. They would not cross the line even for the many seed pods in the sun. They knew they were safer in the dim corner of the church wing.

The psalmist had also seen birds in the shadow of the temple. He may have seen mother birds raise their wings to shade their chicks. Perhaps he noticed the young birds hiding under the mother's outstretched feathers when a hawk swept by.

The psalmist also had trouble with his enemies. In the light of what he saw he felt safe in the shadow of God's ''wings.''

We probably would rather not admit it, but we must admit that we too have enemies! Sometimes they threaten us. Then God's care and concern become a hiding place for us. We find a new confidence in the overshadowing closeness of God.

We confess, O Father, that sometimes we are afraid. Maybe right now we fear we have no protection from our foes. Help us to find security in you. Cover us with your shadow. In Christ. Amen.

Read Matthew 2: 13–15.

SAVED BY A DREAM

**"Rise, take the child and his mother, and flee to Egypt."
Matthew 2: 13.**

Joseph responded by saying yes to his dreams. In a dream he was told to defy convention and marry a woman who was pregnant with a child he did not father. Had he "divorced her quietly," he would have lost his happiness with Mary, his beloved, and his destiny as Mary's husband.

Again, had he returned to his hometown, he likely would have lost the life of the infant Jesus. Responding to a dream, Joseph saved his life and the child's from the massacre prompted by Herod's madness.

"Is not life more than food, and the body more than clothing?" Jesus asked. (Matt. 6: 25) He constantly called his disciples to a realization that life is creative, purposeful, consecrated to God's unfolding plan for creation.

How much of your life is lived in response to convention, tradition, doing what is expected and what has always been? How much is lived in response to God's call to make the world what it ought to be? There always have been those who have looked after themselves, hated their enemies, looked out for number one. Maybe the kingdom of God is the place where people live their dreams instead of surrendering to the sameness of tradition.

Gracious God, grant us blindness to the "common sense" that says "we cannot"; and openness to the vision that begins, "Follow me." Amen.

THOSE WHO STAY WITH THE STUFF

For as his share is who goes down into the battle, so shall his share be who stays by the baggage.
1 Samuel 30: 24.

The King James Version translates the above verse to read: "But as his part *is* that goeth down to the battle, so *shall* his part *be* that tarrieth by the stuff." David, the respected speaker, was saying that the work done by the soldiers at the front lines in front of all who cared to look was no more important than the work of those who stayed behind with the stuff! Baggage tenders, cooks, armor-repairers, and who knows what else? But they're important enough to share equally in the rewards of victory.

I've had people say to me, "But you're a preacher! You're a teacher! I'm only a grocery store clerk, or a filling station attendent, or a common laborer. You're the one doing God's work." Oh no! We *all* are doing God's work. God blesses those who labor by staying with the stuff just as he does the headliners. And we share the fruit of our successes now just as we will share God's eternal rewards. If you earn your bread by "staying with the stuff," believe truly that you are pleasing in God's sight.

Our Lord and Savior, you know the significance of all occupations, whether we call them great or small! Help us to see how closely tied to one another we really are and how important it is to "stay by the stuff." Amen.

Read Matthew 9: 35–38.

HARASSED AND HELPLESS

When he saw the crowds, he had compassion for them, because they were harassed and helpless.
Matthew 9: 36.

There is a dark side to our world, a dark that is ominous and cruel beyond measure or imagination. As I write these meditations in the safety and comfort of my study, millions are dead in Cambodia and more will die in the months to come. There will be no reprieve. Such human tragedy in a society that knows such wealth and pleasure is beyond us.

But, according to all we have been told, we are summoned to carry the cross after the example of Jesus, into the world, following a way that leads ever more deeply into the night. It is in the dark night that we truly know a faith that leads out of darkness.

So if the church is to understand the whole human situation, if we are to speak to it with any meaning and integrity, we must be willing to enter into the world's pain and take it into ourselves. However often the church may be wracked with pain in its own body and life, it is always called to share and live the message of God's love for the world. Faith that struggles with darkness and doubt rests on firmer foundations than blind acceptance that all is well in the world. There must always be those who look out into the dark in order to see and hear that God loves the world. Every bit of it! Every person in it!

Give me eyes to see, Lord, ears to hear, Lord, hands to serve, Lord, and a heart to love, Lord. Amen.

Read Genesis 25: 27–34.
FAILING THE TEST

Esau said, "I am about to die; of what use is a birthright to me?"
Genesis 25: 32.

A growling stomach was more important to Esau than a birthright. He failed the test because he allowed immediate satisfaction to take precedence over abiding worth.

The birthright belonged to the firstborn, and although Jacob and Esau were twins, Esau had emerged first and so had the right to be head of the family.

This was more than privilege. It was responsibility: the promise to Abraham was to be passed on to Esau that his family would be a blessing to the whole earth. For the sake of physical satisfaction Esau turned his back on his high calling in God.

We are heirs of God's promise too. The church is called to be the instrument of God's purpose, to be Christ's ambassador. But the spirit of Esau is not dead.

How often the restraints and disciplines required in such a high calling are shrugged off. How frequently those who profess loyalty to the church and what it stands for are among the absent when it interferes with their plans and needs.

"Of what use is a birthright" if it makes me suffer any deprivation?

And the Christ on the cross turns and looks.

Help me, Lord, help me to be faithful in the time of testing for the sake of him who held nothing back, Jesus my Lord. Amen.

Read Genesis 32: 22–31.

REAPING BLESSINGS FROM FAILURES

Jacob was left alone; and a man wrestled with him until the breaking of the day. . . . Jacob said, "I will not let you go, unless you bless me."
Genesis 32:24, 26.

Guilt and fear at midnight! A man's past was about to catch up with him. Esau lay in wait with four hundred men. The outward crisis, as so often happens, produced an inner conflict. In Jacob's own conscience he was facing up to the kind of man he was.

His contestant was God. When the results of moral wrongdoing catch up with us, whatever the immediate confrontation may be, the ultimate antagonist is God. "Against thee, thee only, have I sinned" (Ps. 51:4).

The greatness of Jacob lay in the fact that he was determined that his struggle with guilt and fear should be made into a positive value. "I will not let you go, unless you bless me."

This is the glory of God. God is able to take our failure and sin and weave them into a pattern for good if only we will believe and surrender. Moral disobedience leaves scars, symbolized by Jacob's limp. But through the transforming power and love of God we can be made into greater people not in spite of, but *because of* our failures. God can transform our evil into ultimate good.

Let me always believe, Lord, that the power that raised up Christ Jesus from the dead can raise me up to newness of life, transforming shame into blessing. Through Jesus my Lord. Amen.

Read Luke 15: 11-24.

WHO ARE YOU REALLY?

**"And he arose and came to his father. But while he was yet
at a distance, his father saw him and had compassion,
and ran and embraced him and kissed him."
Luke 15: 20.**

"What a good man!" they may have said of this father,
when he gave his son a small fortune. That was not neces-
sarily true. But the father did show his goodness when he
had compassion on the prodigal.

That helps me see one of the economic principles of
compassionate living: *my identity is not determined by
what I own, by what I spend, or even by what I give.*

"She sold a million dollars' worth of insurance last
year—she's really good." A very good insurance agent
clearly, but really *good,* really happy, really a blessing to
the world, really a child of God? The million-dollar-year
doesn't answer these questions.

"He's really great; he bought his family a house at the
beach." A wealthy man, obviously, but really *great* in the
eyes of his wife, his children, his employees, his God? The
beach house doesn't answer these questions.

Who I am is determined by my response in faith to the
saving love of Jesus Christ, and by my compassion to others flowing from that commitment. Money owned, spent,
or even given simply is not the measure.

O God our Father, we know better, but it's so easy to value
ourselves and others in dollars. Teach us a more excellent
way. In Christ's name. Amen.

THE MIRACLE OF TOUCH

**[Jesus] stretched out his hand and touched him.
Matthew 8: 3.**

A friend of mine who has been speechless since birth, has the most wonderful gift of touch! With a well-placed hand, she conveys tenderness, gives encouragement, imparts sympathy, or expresses love or gratitude. Through her I have learned the eloquent language of touch.

The ways to touch another human being are countless. We can reach out and touch another by a phone call or a letter, by remembering a birthday, or just by a smile. Or, like my friend, with a pat on the shoulder or a gentle touch on the arm, we can give support or love.

A touch can span generations or even oceans to encompass nations. How often, I wonder, could a handshake between leaders have stopped or prevented an international crisis?

The need to touch and be touched is a basic human need. Often the bible tells us that Jesus' followers longed to touch and be touched by him . . . "She said to herself, 'If I only touch his garment'" (Matt. 9: 21). "He came and took her by the hand and lifted her up" (Mark 1: 31). "He took [the children] in his arms and blessed them, laying his hands upon them" (Mark 10: 16).

Yes, Jesus touched; and with his love and blessings, he continues to touch us today. As we reach out toward another, we are ultimately touching him back.

Lord, we feel the touch of your Spirit, in love. Show us how to touch others with your love. Amen.

Read Titus 2: 11-14

THE GIFT ITSELF

**For the grace of God has appeared for the salvation of all.
Titus 2: 11.**

Christmas without garlanded trees and shopping sprees? Without Wise Men, shepherds, angels, stables, and stars? Impossible! Christmas *is* all these things. Take them away and what would Christmas be?

The first Christians knew nothing of these things. They knew only that God had come in Jesus Christ. They knew the incarnation. Perhaps they knew more of Christmas than we do.

The Letter to Titus speaks the Christmas message in its uncluttered essence: "the grace of God has appeared for the salvation of all." Put this way, an idea turns into the real thing! A concept becomes a concrete and personal reality! It is God in Christ who is that grace of God.

We often lament, "Look what the world has come to!" Here we find the New Testament shouting, "Look what has come to the world!"

This is what Christmas means when we tear away the traditions that wrap it and find the gift himself.

Help us, O God, giver of all good gifts, to revel not in the wrappings, but in the great gift you give us in your Son, Jesus Christ our Lord. Call us to celebrate your Son's birth and the great love divine he brings into the world and to each of us. Amen.